the american negro

By

Dr. Lulamae Clemons
Director of Health Education
Riverside County Public Schools
Riverside, California

Dr. Erwin Hollitz
Assistant Superintendent, Curriculum
Alvord School District
Riverside, California

Dr. Gordon Gardner
Director of Research
Riverside County Public Schools
Riverside, California

CALIFORNIA STATE SERIES
Published by
CALIFORNIA STATE DEPARTMENT OF EDUCATION
Sacramento, 1967

TABLE OF CONTENTS

Preface

The Negro Comes to America 1

The Plantation System 4

Seeking Freedom From Slavery 8

Slavery Abolished 14

The Negro Seeks Citizenship 17

Separate But Equal 22

Securing an Education 27

One of the most exciting changes taking place in America today is occurring in the life of the American Negro. Negroes are voting in greater numbers each year. They are seeking and finding new opportunities for earning a living. They are obtaining new educational experiences. They are traveling more, and establishing homes in all regions of our country. For the Negro in America, new frontiers are opening as he seeks full citizenship rights in our country.

This quest for equality under the law by America's 19 million Negroes is one of the dominant themes in the United States during the 1960s. When you realize that about one out of every ten persons in our country is an American Negro seeking his constitutional rights in each of our fifty states, you may understand the importance of knowing more about him.

Although Negroes play an important part in present-day America, they have also played an important role in our nation's past. It is probable that a Negro was with Columbus when he discovered America. Negroes have served and are now serving our national defense program. They contributed greatly to economic development of the agricultural South. In science, their discoveries and inventions have contributed to health, business, and industry. In music, Negro rhythms and melodies have become America's music. In our government, questions relating to Negroes have resulted in famous proclamations, laws, and even amendments to our Federal Constitution. The role of the Negro in America's history has been and still is a significant one.

SPECIAL ACKNOWLEDGMENTS

The authors gratefully acknowledge the help and assistance rendered by the National Association for the Advancement of Colored People and the Association for the Study of Negro Life and History. Both organizations readily responded to all queries and then provided much information used in the text.

The authors also wish to express their appreciation to all those who spent hours of their time in reviewing the manuscript, and who provided many valuable suggestions. Special thanks go to Mrs. Juanita Harris, Consultant, Office of Los Angeles County Superintendent of Schools; Miss Helen Hefferman, Chief, Bureau of Elementary Education, California State Department of Education; Dr. Howardine Hoffman, Director of Elementary Education, Office of Los Angeles County Superintendent of Schools; Dr. John A. Morsell, Assistant to Executive Secretary Roy Wilkins, NAACP; Mr. Wilson Riles, Consultant, California State Department of Education; Mr. Joe Severns, Consultant, Office of Los Angeles County Superintendent of Schools; Dr. Fannie Shaftel, Professor, Stanford University; Dr. Charles Wesley, President, Central State College, Wilberforce, Ohio; Mr. John Reuss, Teaching Assistant, History Department, University of California of Riverside; and Mr. Herbert M. Frisby, Chairman, Matthew Henson Commemorative Projects, Baltimore, Maryland.

The superior numbers which appear in the text are keyed to references listed in the back of the book beginning on page 122. Each reference is listed under the title of the section in which it occurs.

The Negro Comes To America

EARLY EXPLORATIONS

Although it is not known with certainty that African Negroes were in America during the centuries before Columbus, early Indian carvings that resemble Negro faces seem to suggest that this is a strong possibility. There is also some evidence to indicate that the pilot of Columbus's flagship, the *Santa Maria,* was a Negro, Pedro Alonzo Niño. It is known that a Negro named Estéban accompanied the Spanish explorer, Cabeza de Vaca, during his wanderings (1528-1534) from Florida into Mexico. Later, Estéban (Big Steve) guided 600 men across Texas into Arizona and New Mexico. Negroes shared in the Spanish founding of St. Augustine, the first city in America. They were with Ponce de León during his search for a "fountain of youth"; they were with Coronado in New Mexico; and they were with De Soto exploring on the Mississippi.

FROM INDENTURED SERVANT TO SLAVE

The first group of Negroes was brought to the English colonies by the Dutch in 1619. These twenty Negroes worked as indentured servants on the plantations of Virginia. Indentured servants were bound by contract to work for a certain period, usually five to seven years. During this period, they worked for their food, clothing, and shelter. Indentured servants could be traded or sold by their masters. At the end of their contract, however, they were usually given *freedom dues* in the form of a small amount of money, clothing, land, tools, or livestock. They were then free to earn their own living in whatever manner they chose.

As the colonies grew and prospered, the need for labor increased rapidly. Since indentured servants could not be forced to provide free labor after their contracts expired, the colonists resorted to slaves as a more permanent solution to their labor problem. By the second half of the seventeenth century, Negroes were being brought to America as slaves rather than as indentured servants. By 1661, slavery was legalized in the British colonies, and by 1726, British slave trade ships were bringing as many as 100,000 captive slaves to America each year.

SLAVERY IN OTHER LANDS

The practice of one people making slaves of another did not originate in America. It had been a common practice for a conquering people to enslave members of conquered tribes or nations. For the most part, however, the slaves and slave owners were of the same race. Notable examples of large-scale slavery date back centuries before the time of Columbus. During the period of Rome's supremacy in Europe, it is estimated that one-third of Rome's one million inhabitants were slaves. Many of these slaves were natives of Greece.

The movement for enslavement of Negroes originated with the Arabs when they spread across North Africa and onto the Iberian Peninsula during the eighth century. It was not until the fifteenth century

2

(about 1442) that Portugal started the maritime slave trade. By 1460, Portugal was importing substantial numbers of Negro slaves from the west coast of Africa. Most of these slaves were put to work on large estates or were employed as domestic servants in the cities and towns. Some slaves were sold in Spain where they were used in a similar fashion.

It is difficult to determine with any accuracy the number of slaves imported into Portugal and Spain during the fifteenth century. But we do know that both countries had an appreciable slave population at the time of Columbus's first voyage.

THE UNITED STATES PROHIBITS
THE IMPORTATION OF SLAVES

The importation of slaves by Americans continued through the colonial period. After the Revolution, the Federal Congress in 1808 made it illegal to bring slaves into the United States. However, this did not completely stop the selling of Africans into slavery. Many of them were still kidnapped and smuggled into Southern ports as late as 1859. The large plantations of the South required a large supply of labor. It was difficult for the Federal government to stop the smuggling of slaves. In many of the ports of the South, smuggling was either tolerated by the authorities, or it was carried on secretly at night.

It should be noted that a number of Africans sold into slavery were well educated for their day, including some who spoke Arabic, the language of the scholars in northern and western Africa. It is only fair to point out, however, that most of the slaves could neither read nor write. Their native village life did not require the use of a written language.

The Plantation System

THE PLANTATION

Slavery in America was centered in the plantation system, which had its origin in the West Indies. The word *plantation* means a farm or estate where something is planted. While most Southern plantations were small, others were vast tracts of land comprising thousands of acres. Many plantation owners were wealthy, aristocratic gentlemen who exported large quantities of tobacco, rice, or cotton. Plantations were largely self-sufficient communities that produced virtually all the necessities of life. Tools that could not be manufactured locally, and also most luxuries, were imported from England. Many plantations had stores, mills, tanneries, wood and metal shops, stables, wharves, and warehouses.

As pointed out earlier, plantation owners first used indentured servants to supply their labor needs. As the demand for America's tobacco and cotton increased and more plantation land was brought under cultivation to meet this demand, the plantation owners turned to the slave system to fill their labor needs.

LIFE ON THE PLANTATION

Life for most Negroes on a plantation revolved around the raising of cotton, tobacco, rice, and sugar

4

The beautifully designed ironwork on these older buildings in New Orleans is an example of the Negro ironsmith's skill.

cane. They were forced to work at clearing the land, plowing, planting, cultivating, harvesting, and preparing the crops for market. Men, women, and children alike were forced to work in the fields.

Most Negroes were field hands, but some worked as carpenters, blacksmiths, brickmasons, harnessmakers, candlemakers, jewelers, printers, ironsmiths, painters, mechanics, cabinetmakers, bakers, chefs, porters, housemaids, dairymaids, teachers, or governesses. Some slaves developed prized skills in these areas of work. The fine, complicated iron work of the Negro still can be seen in many areas of the South.

The master's house on a plantation was often a white pillared mansion with elegant, imported furnishings. Negro families usually lived in pine board shanties at the rear of the master's house. The Negroes who lived in more comfortable quarters worked very closely with the master and his family and had a higher social status than the field workers. Servants enjoyed special privileges. They received better food, finer clothes, and obtained travel opportunities not generally given to lower-status persons.

Religion played an important role in the lives of many Negroes. In early colonial times, Negro and white persons often worshiped together. This practice declined, but a few privileged servants often continued to worship with the master's family. In time there developed a practice of segregation—the complete separation of the races. Thus on Sunday mornings, Negroes came together to worship by themselves. Out of these gatherings developed a highly spiritual religion. Today, the songs that were introduced during these services form an important part of our cultural heritage. These highly spiritual hymns reflected not only the slaves' hopes but their hardships as well.

TREATMENT OF THE SLAVES

The masters of plantations did not all have the same attitude toward their slaves. At one extreme, the master treated his slaves with kindness and was concerned about their welfare.

In contrast to the friendly and helpful behavior of some masters, others gave scant attention to the problems and interests of Negro families. Life was especially difficult for the Negro when he was directed by a harsh overseer. The overseer, usually a white man, managed and directed the operation of some or all phases of plantation production. Because it was the overseer's responsibility to make the plantation a profitable business, he often worked the slaves too hard and too long without regard for their health or well-being. It was not uncommon for some slaves to work an eighteen-hour day. For the vast majority of slaves, plantation life was just plain hard work.

FREEDOM: A GOAL TO SEEK

Regardless of whether the master or overseer was friendly or unfriendly, slaves could not call their lives their own. They could not participate in government. They could not own land. They could not travel from place to place. In many Southern states, laws forbade the education of Negroes, both slave and free. Moreover, members of families were usually separated when sold at the slave market.

Although some Negroes accepted the condition of slavery and the plantation life to which they were tied, many rebelled against this bondage and sought their freedom by escape to the free states of the North.

Seeking Freedom From Slavery

"Poets, with voices of melody, sing for freedom. Who could tune for slavery?"

—CHARLES SUMNER
Speech in the Senate, 1852

DOORS TO FREEDOM

During the 240 years of bondage in America, thousands of Negro slaves desperately wanted their freedom. However, freedom was not easy to obtain. Some of the slaves managed to buy their freedom or pay "escape money." To obtain money some slaves worked as part-time laborers for other planters and townspeople who needed extra help. Some slaves, with the consent of their masters, worked as craftsmen and sold their handiwork to planters and merchants. It often took a slave years to earn the price of his freedom. A few masters did free their slaves because they did not believe that one man should be a slave to another. For example, George Washington's will provided freedom for all his slaves upon the death of Mrs. Washington. Most slaves, however, could not escape or obtain freedom from servitude.

Great risks were involved whenever the slave sought his freedom by attempting to escape. Despite the risks, many thousands of them attempted to run away from their owners. Some of them managed to outwit the manhunters and dogs used to track them down, and escaped into the swamps and forests to live with friendly Indians.

THE UNDERGROUND RAILROAD

One of the most successful methods established to help Negroes escape to freedom was the *Underground Railroad,* a series of secret routes to the North and to Canada. These routes were organized and operated by persons who wished to see slavery abolished because they believed it was wrong to keep anyone in bondage. Between 1830 and 1860, over 50,000 slaves escaped to freedom by traveling along the 1,000 routes of the Underground Railroad. Fugitives received rest, food, and shelter during the day, and they were conducted from "station to station" at night.

In the decades before the Civil War, many brave people helped others escape. One notable example was a former slave named Harriet Tubman who worked with the Underground Railroad. She escaped from bondage in Maryland when this work began. Between secret rescue missions into the South, Mrs. Tubman made anti-slavery speeches in the North to secure support for the abolition of slavery. During the Civil War, she nursed Union Soldiers and served as an army scout and intelligence agent. She carried out dangerous missions behind the Confederate lines and once carried out large-scale sabotage against Confederate military supplies. It is amazing that an illiterate former slave could have done so much for the cause of freedom.

William Still was chairman of the
Philadelphia branch of the Underground Railroad from 1851 to
1861. Still sheltered the family of
John Brown while he was awaiting
execution in Virginia.

The Associated Publishers, Inc.

The Associated Publishers, Inc.

Robert Purvis, a wealthy abolitionist and resident of Philadelphia,
was president of the Underground
Railroad which was established in
1838.

The Associated Publishers, Inc.

Isabella Hardenburgh, born a slave
in Ulster County, New York, but
freed by state law in 1827, was
an ardent abolitionist. After a religious experience she took the
name of Sojourner Truth by which
she is best remembered.

10

Harriet Tubman helped to free over three hundred slaves and contributed much to the Union cause. This is but one example of the many valiant efforts to help others achieve a freedom that was taken for granted by millions of people. Truly people like Harriet Tubman were in the vanguard of those fighting for freedom, and they contributed much to the growth of democracy in our country.

In the hope of easing the mounting tension over the slavery question, Congress passed a series of laws which became known as the Compromise of 1850. One of the laws was a new and more drastic Fugitive Slave Law, providing for Federal assistance in capturing and returning slaves to their owners. Many people in the North chose to ignore the provisions of the law, however, and it was virtually impossible to enforce it. But escape was not easy, even with the help of the Abolitionists, who advocated immediate freedom for the slaves. Many thousands of runaway slaves were captured and severely punished by their masters. Those slaves who did escape fled mostly to the large cities of the North.

SLAVES RESORT TO ARMED REBELLION

In some instances slaves openly rebelled against their owners. Armed rebellion was tried in several states, but it always failed. One such violent insurrection occurred in Virginia in 1831. Nat Turner, a Negro preacher, led about sixty armed slaves in an attack on plantations. More than fifty white persons lost their lives before the rebellion was crushed. Nat Turner and nineteen of his companions were executed for treason.

The most famous rebellion against the slave owners was led by John Brown, a religious fanatic who believed that he had a divine mission to free the slaves. On

October 16, 1859, John Brown and a small group of followers attacked and easily occupied the Federal arsenal at Harpers Ferry, Virginia. In addition, Brown's force captured some sixty citizens of Harpers Ferry and held them as hostages. Two days later, a force of marines under Colonel Robert E. Lee broke into the arsenal and captured Brown. A short time later, Brown was tried for treason and was hanged.

Desperate rebellions like those led by Nat Turner and John Brown were scattered and not well organized. They did, however, serve to focus public attention on the slaves' burning desire for freedom.

THE FREE NEGRO

Up to this point, we have been discussing some ways by which slaves sought to obtain their freedom. It should be recalled that during these times there were many Negroes who were already free. In 1800, there were approximately 100,000 free Negroes. By 1860, this number had risen to nearly 500,000. It is rather surprising to learn that more than one-half of these free Negroes lived in the Southern states.

Probably the first free Negroes were those who completed the terms of their indenture contracts in the 1600s. When indentures were paid in full, it was possible for them to live as free men. As time passed, other Negroes succeeded in obtaining their freedom. Since the law provided that children of a free mother were also free, some Negroes were born free. Others purchased their freedom from agreeable masters. Some slaves obtained freedom by an act called *manumission,* that is, the master legally granted freedom to his slaves. Additional thousands gained their freedom by fleeing to free states.

Citizenship of the free Negro was a puzzling problem. Generally, in the South, he could not vote, serve on juries, or hold public office. He was frequently required to identify himself as a free person so that he would not be seized as a fugitive slave. He was free to own property and even own slaves. He was obliged to pay taxes, and he could engage in business enterprises. At times, free Negroes appealed to the courts and received the same justice that all citizens might expect. More often, however, it was impossible for them to obtain equal justice under the law. Often they were punished for offenses as though they were slaves.

In brief, the free Negro was not always free in the fullest sense of the term. What actually happened to him often depended upon a particular situation. In other words, he was the subject of prejudices and discrimination and could never be sure of his business or social relationship with other persons.

Slavery Abolished

"In giving freedom to the slave, we assure freedom to the free."

—ABRAHAM LINCOLN

THE EMANCIPATION PROCLAMATION

In 1862, President Abraham Lincoln announced that unless those states that had seceded from the Union ceased their "rebellion" by January 1, 1863, the slaves in those states would be declared free. Consequently, on January 1, 1863, Lincoln issued his famous Emancipation Proclamation. This proclamation did not immediately free any slaves. Only those slaves held in territory controlled by the Confederacy were included under the proclamation. Before these slaves could be freed, however, the Union forces had to wrest control of the territory from the Confederates.

That portion of the Emancipation Proclamation which dealt with the freeing of slaves and the position of the Federal executive regarding them follows:

That on the first day of January, in the year of our Lord one thousand eight hundred and sixty-three, all persons held as slaves within any state or designated part of a state, the people whereof shall then be in rebellion against the United States, shall be then, thenceforward, and forever free; and the Executive Government of the United States, including the military and naval authority thereof, will recognize and maintain the freedom of such persons, and will do no act or acts to repress such persons, or any of them, in any efforts they may make for their actual freedom.

It was not until 1865 that all Negro slaves were officially freed. This came as a result of the Thirteenth Amendment to our Constitution which states in part, "neither slavery nor involuntary servitude . . . shall exist within the United States, or any place subject to their jurisdiction." This act applied to all slaves in our country, regardless of the states in which they lived.

THE PROBLEMS OF FREEDOM

Can you imagine the different thoughts and problems these former slaves had when they realized they were free? After years of slavery, it must have been difficult for them to assume so suddenly the responsibilities of free men and women. Now they were faced with such problems as securing a living, providing a home, helping the family stay together, educating the children, and living as free persons.

Even today such complicated concepts as freedom and responsibility are not fully understood by all Americans. What could "freedom" mean to the recently freed Negro who had never been free? What could "responsibility" mean to a people who had rarely been allowed to make decisions or had seldom been given a choice in running their own affairs? No other group of Americans has ever had to face such a complex situation. To whom could the Negro turn for advice?

Who would be willing to help him learn to use his newly acquired freedom and responsibilities to the best advantage? These were indeed difficult times for the Negro.

FREEDOM: THE FIRST STEP TOWARD CITIZENSHIP

Although the Thirteenth Amendment to the Constitution granted legal freedom to all slaves, the road to full citizenship rights has been long and strewn with obstacles. As pointed out previously, the fact that a Negro was legally freed under the Constitution did not mean that he had all the rights and privileges accorded a citizen of the United States. State and local laws have been used to deprive him of his civil and political rights. Discrimination and prejudice have prevented full realization of his economic potential. One hundred years have passed since the Thirteenth Amendment became a part of our Constitution, and full citizenship for all is still a goal to be achieved.

The Negro
Seeks Citizenship

*"All persons born or naturalized in the United
States, and subject to the jurisdiction thereof,
are citizens of the United States . . ."*

—FOURTEENTH AMENDMENT
Constitution of the United States

THE FOURTEENTH AMENDMENT

Although the slaves were freed by the Thirteenth
Amendment, they were not granted legal citizenship
until the Fourteenth Amendment became part of the
Constitution in 1868. This amendment guaranteed citizenship to all persons born in the United States or
who became citizens by naturalization. Until the Fourteenth Amendment, citizenship had not been defined
in the Constitution. Under this amendment, all former
slaves, as well as all other persons born in the United
States automatically became citizens of the United
States and the states where they lived.

Now that citizenship was granted to all native-born
or naturalized persons, Negroes meeting either of these

qualifications could no longer be lawfully deprived of life, liberty, or property without due process of law. The Fourteenth Amendment served as the legal basis upon which the courts of the United States guaranteed rights that might otherwise be denied to the Negro. If rights were denied, the Federal courts could be called upon to judge the validity of the complaint. Despite the Fourteenth Amendment, however, many Negroes were frequently denied their citizenship rights by state laws enacted for that purpose.

SECURING THE RIGHT TO VOTE

Although the Fourteenth Amendment provided for Negro citizenship, it remained for the Fifteenth Amendment, which became part of the Constitution in 1870, to forbid denying the right to vote to any citizen "on account of race, color, or previous condition of servitude." It is important to remember, however, that each individual state has the right to decide on the qualifications of its citizens to vote. During the years since the founding of our government, the voting requirements within the various states have changed. For the most part, however, a minimum age, a specific length of time as a resident of the state, and proper registration have been the basic requirements.

Following the Civil War, some states established voting requirements that effectively prevented most Negroes from voting. For example, before being permitted to vote citizens had to (1) prove that they were able to read and write and to interpret the Constitution, (2) own property, and (3) pay a sum of money—a poll tax. Since many Negroes could not read or write, did not own property, and had little money they were not permitted to vote. Whether a citizen fulfilled the provision concerning the interpretation of the Constitution was determined by the person in charge of voter registration. Consequently, this device was used to prevent Negroes from voting. Although these requirements applied to all persons, they worked more against Negroes than against white persons.

In addition to the legal devices, economic pressures and outright physical intimidation were frequently used to prevent Negroes from voting.

RECENT EFFORTS TO GUARANTEE VOTING RIGHTS

Approximately ten million American Negroes would be eligible to vote if all were permitted to register. But many Negroes are not permitted to register. Since exercising the right to vote can be one of the most important ways for all persons to obtain citizenship rights in our country, Negro leaders are placing more emphasis on the problem of registration than ever before.

Although the increased emphasis on voting registration is of recent origin, there has been a rather surprising increase in the number of Negro registrations since 1920. In ten states of the South, the number of Negroes registered to vote increased from about 70,000 in 1920 to approximately 1,500,000 in 1962.[1]

In an effort to make it possible for all qualified persons to vote, Congress has passed a series of civil rights laws. In 1957, Congress passed and President Dwight D. Eisenhower signed a Civil Rights Act which provides for Federal enforcement of those civil rights guaranteed by the Constitution. This legislation included the following provisions:

1. The Attorney General, acting for the United States, was given power to secure court orders that would

prevent local voting officials from denying the right to register or vote to properly qualified persons.

2. A Commission on Civil Rights, appointed by the President with the consent of the Senate, was established with authority to investigate registration and voting practices in local areas.

3. The Federal district courts were empowered to decide whether local officials were correct when they refused any person the right to register or to vote.

In 1960, an expanded Civil Rights Act further provided that (1) the Federal courts could appoint referees with authority to issue voting certificates and (2) state election officials be required to keep all voting records available for inspection for a period of twenty-two months following a primary or general election.

The importance of these civil rights laws may be seen from the fact that in one local area some 1,300 Negroes had their voting rights restored after their names had been removed from the list of registered voters.

In 1962, Congress passed and sent to the states for ratification a constitutional amendment which provided that a citizen's right to vote shall not be denied for failure to pay a poll tax or any other kind of tax. In January, 1964, North Dakota became the thirty-eighth state to ratify the so-called poll tax proposal, and it became the Twenty-fourth Amendment to the Constitution. It should be noted, however, that this amendment applies only to Federal elections.

Further protection of voting rights for Negroes, as well as for all citizens, is provided in the Civil Rights Act of 1964. The provisions of this act are summarized in the Appendix.

The right of the Negro to vote is important not only to him but also to our country. You can realize the importance of his vote when you recall that about one out of every ten persons in the United States is a Negro.

Since World War II, the size of the Negro vote has increased significantly. This increase is due to (1) the increase in Negro population; (2) an increase in the number of Negroes owning property; (3) the development of organizations to work for Negro rights; (4) Negroes becoming more actively interested in the political affairs of the nation; (5) the Negro's increasing awareness of the responsibilities of full citizenship; and (6) Federal laws to protect the voting rights of all people. As the full force of these factors comes into play, we can confidently expect the Negro vote to become an increasingly important element in all our elections.

Separate But Equal

"On this generation of Americans falls the burden of proving to the world that we really mean it when we say all men are created free and equal before the law."

—ROBERT KENNEDY
United States Attorney General

PLESSY V. FERGUSON

In 1896, the Supreme Court decision in the case of *Plessy v. Ferguson* held that an 1890 Louisiana statute requiring railroads to provide separate but equal travel accommodations for Caucasian and Negro passengers did not constitute a denial of equal protection of the law. Homer Plessy, who was regarded as a Negro, purchased a ticket to travel between two cities in Louisiana. Upon boarding the train, he entered a coach reserved for Caucasian passengers. The conductor asked Plessy to move into a section reserved for Negro passengers. When Plessy refused to give up his seat, he was arrested and charged with violation of the statute. Plessy and his lawyer carried the case to the Supreme Court in order to challenge the constitutionality of the Louisiana statute. The Supreme Court consented to review the case and subsequently upheld the con-

22

stitutionality of the Louisiana law. The Court's decision was an interpretation of this clause of the Fourteenth Amendment:

> No state shall make or enforce any law which shall abridge the privileges or immunities of citizens of the United States; nor shall any state deprive any person of life, liberty or property, without due process of law; nor deny to any person within its jurisdiction the equal protection of the laws.

The Court said that Louisiana's requirement of separate but equal facilities did not necessarily imply inferiority of the Negroes and, therefore, did not violate the "equal protection of the laws" guarantee of the Fourteenth Amendment. Thus the Supreme Court decision in *Plessy v. Ferguson* legally established the "separate but equal" doctrine that was to continue for almost sixty years.

As it turned out, much more was involved in the *Plessy* decision than where a man should sit on a train. The principle established by the Court's decision was gradually extended into many phases of living—separate schools, separate community recreational resources, separate transportation, separate accommodations, and separate housing.

JUSTICE HARLAN DISSENTS

One member of the Supreme Court, Justice John Harlan, wrote a dissenting opinion in the *Plessy* case:

> In respect of civil rights, common to all citizens, the Constitution of the United States does not, I think, permit any public authority to know the race of those entitled to be protected in the enjoyment of such rights . . . I deny that any legislative body or judicial tribunal may have

regard to the race of citizens when the civil rights of those citizens are involved . . .

The law regards man as man, and takes no account of his surroundings or of his color when his civil rights as guaranteed by the Supreme Law of the land are involved . . .

The arbitrary separation of citizens, on the basis of race, while they are on a public highway, is a badge of servitude wholly inconsistent with the civil freedom and the equality before the law established by the Constitution. It cannot be justified upon any legal grounds.[1]

Although Justice Harlan's dissenting opinion did not change the Supreme Court ruling, his interpretation did give expression to a point of view that was to prevail many years later.

TRUMAN CREATES A COMMITTEE ON CIVIL RIGHTS

In 1946, President Harry Truman used his Presidential power to issue Executive Order 9908 which provided for the formation of a committee to be known as the President's Committee on Civil Rights. The purpose of this Committee was to make recommendations for revitalizing and protecting the civil rights of citizens as guaranteed by the United States Constitution. Specifically, the Committee was to make recommendations as to ways in which law-enforcement agencies of Federal, state, and local governments could strengthen and safeguard the civil rights of citizens in such matters as voting, housing, working, and traveling in all parts of the United States. This Committee was terminated after reporting to the President. Although its recommendations were not enacted into law, they did serve to focus attention on the problem.

THE COMMISSION ON CIVIL RIGHTS

Eleven years after President Truman's Executive Order of 1946, the United States Commission on Civil Rights, mentioned in the previous section, was created by the Civil Rights Act of 1957. The purpose of the Commission, a bipartisan agency, was and still is to study civil rights problems and report its findings to the President and Congress. Briefly, the Commission's function remains one of advising the President and Congress on conditions that may deprive American citizens of equal treatment under the law because of their color, creed, religion, or national origin. The power of the Commission is limited to making studies, collecting data, and evaluating information relating to civil rights. This information may then be used for either executive or legislative action.

The Civil Rights Commission has no power to enforce laws or correct any individual wrong. Originally, the Commission was created for a two-year period, from 1957 through 1959, but Congress has kept the Commission active by repeatedly extending its term. The present term runs through January, 1968. In 1959, the Commission added to its agenda the study of government-contract employment and the administration of justice. The membership of the Commission includes and has included some of this nation's most competent educators, legal authorities, and government administrators.

CIVIL RIGHTS MOVE AHEAD

In addition to the Civil Rights Acts and the Civil Rights Commission at the national level, many states have established advisory committees to study problems dealing with civil rights. These committees report their findings and make recommendations to the governments of their respective states.

It is evident that the cause of civil rights has advanced materially since the 1896 Supreme Court decision in the case of *Plessy v. Ferguson*. This has been particularly true since World War II. The separate but equal doctrine, given legal basis by the Court's decision in 1896, would have continued indefinitely had not the Supreme Court reversed its judgment in a later case. The test of the separate but equal doctrine came not over a question of transportation but one concerned with education in the public schools. In 1954, the Supreme Court agreed to review several cases dealing with segregation in public schools. In all of these cases the separate but equal doctrine was the issue.

Securing an Education

"We conclude that in the field of public education the doctrine of 'separate but equal' has no place. Separate educational facilities are inherently unequal."

—THE UNITED STATES SUPREME COURT
Brown v. Board of Education of Topeka (1954)

SEPARATE BUT EQUAL IS REVERSED

The historic Supreme Court decision which declared the separate but equal doctrine unconstitutional came in the case of *Brown v. Board of Education of Topeka, Kansas.* Under this title, the Court combined several school desegregation cases. The Court unanimously ruled that "separate educational facilities are inherently unequal." In essence, this was what a Kansas judge had found to be true, although he ruled against desegregating Kansas schools. The Supreme Court quoted his words in its opinion:

Segregation of the white and colored children in public schools has a detrimental effect upon the colored children. The impact is greater when it has the sanction of the law; for the policy of separating the races is usually interpreted as denoting the inferiority of the Negro group. A sense of inferiority affects the motivation of a child to learn. Segregation with the sanction of law, therefore, has a tendency to retard the educational and mental development of Negro children and to deprive them of some of the benefits they would receive in a racially integrated school system.[1]

SCHOOL DESEGREGATION PROGRESSES SLOWLY

Despite the fact that it has been over ten years since the Supreme Court ordered the integration of all public schools, relatively little progress has been made. Actually, in most cases court action against each school district has been needed to effect school desegregation.

Court procedures take a long time and are extremely expensive. And while the courts have been deciding the legal issues, some people were taking action on their own. Not all of these attempts at school desegregation have been peaceful. Soldiers were required in Little Rock, Arkansas. The riots in Clinton, Tennessee, Birmingham, Alabama, and at the University of Mississippi are not pleasant incidents to remember. But we cannot ignore the facts. The Negro is becoming increasingly determined to achieve those rights that are constitutionally guaranteed every American citizen. The important thing is that cooperation on the part of both Negro and Caucasian leaders is being sought in an effort to prevent additional explosive situations from occurring.

The percentage of Negroes attending schools with Caucasians in the Southern and border states was at a 9.3 percent level by the close of the 1963-64 school year. The chart on the following page gives some of the details in the move toward desegregation in these seventeen Southern and border states and the District of Columbia.

Public School Desegregation[2]

| | School Districts | | | Negroes in Schools With Whites | |
	Total	With Negroes & Whites	Deseg.	No.	Percent
Ala...............	114	114	4	21	.007
Ark...............	415	228	13	366	.327
Fla...............	67	67	16	3,650	1.53
Ga...............	197	181	4	177	.052
La...............	67	67	2	1,814	.602
Miss.............	150	150	0	0	.000
N. C..............	171	171	40	1,865	.537
S. C..............	108	108	1	10	.004
Tenn.............	154	143	45	4,486	2.72
Tex...............1,421	1,421	899	263	18,000	5.52
Va...............	130	128	55	3,721	1.63
SOUTH........2,994	2,994	2,256	443	34,110	1.18
Del...............	86	86	86	10,209	56.5
D. C..............	1	1	1	98,813	83.8
Ky...............	204	165	163	29,855	54.4
Md...............	24	23	23	76,906	47.8
Mo...............1,597	1,597	212	203	40,000	42.1
Okla.............1,160	1,160	241	197	12,289	28.0
W. Va............	55	44	44	13,659	58.2
'BORDER.......3,127	3,127	772	717	281,731	54.8
REGION..........6,121	6,121	3,028	1,160	315,841	9.3

NEGROES SEEK AN EDUCATION

After the Civil War, many Negroes made every effort to acquire further education. By 1900, over one-half of the Negro population could read and write, even though many schools for Negroes were segregated, poorly equipped, and inadequately financed.

Between 1865 and 1880, several schools for Negroes were established either through private funds, the resources of the Federal government, or a combination of private and state funds. Fisk University in Tennessee, Atlanta University in Georgia, and Hampton Institute in Virginia received private funds. Howard University in Washington, D. C. was financed by the

Federal government, and Tuskegee Institute near Tuskegee, Alabama, received a small amount of money ($2,000 a year) from the state of Alabama. Several other schools were made possible through government landgrant financing as provided under the Morrill Act of 1862.

Among those Negroes who were successful in acquiring an education, none was more notable than Booker T. Washington. Born April 5, 1856, in a small cabin in Franklin County, Virginia, Booker T. Washington became a man of historical significance. The first nine years of his life were spent as a slave on a small plantation no different from many others. After the Civil War, he moved to Malden, West Virginia. Here he attended a mission school. In 1872, Booker entered Hampton Institute, a Negro college in Virginia, where he worked as a janitor to help pay for his education.

Following his graduation from Hampton, Booker taught school. In 1881, he was selected to head a new school near Tuskegee, Alabama. This new school (Tuskegee Institute) had two buildings, little money, and very little equipment. If you were to visit the campus of this school today, you would find 160 buildings, 5,000 acres of land, 2,400 students, about 250 faculty members, and an endowment of some 14 million dollars.

During the years since 1881, more than 55,000 students have been enrolled in this institution. Today, the graduates of Tuskegee—teachers, nurses, doctors, veterinarians, engineers, economists, and agriculturists—are to be found in all parts of our country and the world. One of the most famous teachers at Tuskegee was the world renowned scientist, George Washington Carver.

Booker T. Washington died in 1915 and was buried on the campus of the school to which he contributed so much. In 1945, he was elected to the Hall of Fame for Famous Americans, and thirteen years later Congress established his birthplace as a national monument.

During his life, Booker T. Washington founded not only Tuskegee Institute but also a philosophy for many of his people. As one of their leaders, he saw vocational education as a road to economic progress. At the same time, he advised the Negroes not to agitate for racial, civil, and political equality.

Washington's emphasis on vocational education and his submissive policy regarding relations between the races did not go unchallenged. In 1901, opposition to Washington's philosophy broke into the open. The opposition movement under the leadership of two Negroes, William Monroe Trotter of Harvard University and George Forbes of Amherst, held that Washington's teachings were destructive of the Negro's guaranteed rights and privileges. In 1905, the so-called Niagara Movement was launched. This movement was aimed at the elimination of discrimination and advocated full political and civil rights and equal opportunity for higher education. When the National Association for the Advancement of Colored People was organized in 1909, it absorbed virtually the entire membership of the Niagara Movement.

MARY MCLEOD BETHUNE

Perhaps the only school ever founded with an endowment of only one dollar and fifty cents was the Daytona Educational and Industrial Training School.

This school, founded by Mrs. Mary McLeod Bethune, opened during 1904 in Daytona, Florida.

For years Mrs. Bethune had cherished the desire to open a school for the education of girls. She arrived in Daytona with one dollar and fifty cents in her purse, and without a place to live. Mrs. Bethune arranged to rent a cabin, and it was here that five girls enrolled for classes on the day that Mrs. Bethune opened her school. From this humble beginning, the school rose to national prominence because of its excellent program. Its early curriculum included courses in commercial and industrial subjects. Later, teacher training was added when it became an accredited junior college. In 1923, Mrs. Bethune's school merged with Cookman Institute, and thus became a school for both boys and girls. Soon the college had more than fourteen buildings with assets of more than 500,000 dollars.

Plans are being made by the National Council of Negro Women, with the aid of other civic organizations, to erect a Bethune monument and education center in Washington, D. C. The United States Congress has authorized the placement of the Bethune monument in Lincoln Park, where the monument to Abraham Lincoln is located.

NEGRO SCHOOL ATTENDANCE IMPROVES

In the United States today, as in the past, there is the problem of student "drop-outs." In part, this problem results from the attitude, "Why should I stay in school? What good will it do me? I can't get a good position even if I graduate." Today there is reason to believe that this attitude is changing. It is undoubtedly true that discrimination has prevented qualified Negroes from obtaining the better positions. Negro boys and girls are coming to realize, however, that good preparation is essential for obtaining good positions even when discrimination is not a factor. The same is true for any boy or girl, regardless of color or creed. As a result, Negro youths are staying in school for longer periods of time and enrolling in programs of higher education—technical schools, junior colleges, and universities.

Percent of Nonwhites* Enrolled in School 1940-1963

Age	1940[3]	1963[4]
7-13 years	91.2	99.0
14-17 years	68.2	90.4
18-19 years	21.1	39.8
20-24 years	3.8	10.2

*On this chart and those on following pages, Negroes constitute 95 percent of the nonwhite statistics.

In 1950, some 167,200 Negroes had completed four or more years of college work. By 1960, this figure had risen to about 329,650. In addition, Negro enrollments in graduate and professional schools have tripled in the last twenty years. While these figures illustrate significant progress, the Negro is still well behind the American community as a whole.

Today, the young Negro is experiencing new trends and new thoughts about school life and careers in business and industry. He is relating the two—education and securing a living. Both are opening doors to him. Although only about 7 percent of all Negroes in the world live in the United States, there are far more of them in our colleges and universities than there are in all of the other colleges and universities of the world. In addition to the fact that he may now attend nearly all institutions of higher education which denied admission to him prior to the 1954 school desegregation decision, he has available to him about 125 colleges and universities that were originally established for the education of Negroes. The opportunity for him to become educated is limited mainly by his desire and, of course, his ability to succeed and to pay his way. These are problems which all students face.

In addition to the fact that Negro students are now attending colleges and universities formerly closed to them by the separate but equal doctrine, it is interesting to note that Caucasian students are now enrolling at state-supported and private institutions of higher learning originally established for the Negro. Examples include Lincoln University in Jefferson City, Missouri; Howard University in Washington D.C.; and West Virginia State College in Institute, West Virginia.

COLLEGIATE HONORS AND ACHIEVEMENT

While attending institutions of higher learning, the Negro is participating actively in campus life. This participation in many instances has resulted in campus honors.

Julius LaVonne Chambers was selected as editor in chief of the University of North Carolina's *Law Review*. Chambers, a straight "A" student, received this appointment because of his academic excellence, his writing ability, and his above-average performance on the staff of the *Law Review* over a two-year period.

Nancy Streets and Thomas Atkins, Indiana University students, have each earned recognition on campus. Miss Streets was awarded the title of "Miss Indiana University" and Atkins was elected president of the student body.

At the University of California in Los Angeles (UCLA), Rafer Johnson served as student body president during the 1958-59 school year. Johnson, one of the world's greatest all-around track and field performers, climaxed his active athletic career by winning the coveted Decathlon Gold Medal in the 1960 Olympic Games in Rome, Italy. He was further honored by being selected to carry the flag for the United States team in the opening Olympic parade at Rome. Rafer Johnson was the recipient of the James E. Sullivan Trophy as the nation's outstanding amateur athlete of 1960. As a sophomore in 1956, he led the UCLA track team to its first Pacific Coast and National Collegiate Athletic Association track team championship.

Wilma Rudolph, a student at Tennessee Agricultural and Industrial State University, became the first American woman in history to win three gold medals in the Olympic games. At the 1960 Olympics, she electrified the spectators as she won the women's 100-meter and 200-meter dashes. In addition, she anchored the winning 400-meter relay team. Wilma Rudolph's feat was all the more remarkable when you consider the fact that a childhood illness made it impossible for her to walk until she was eight years old.

Earl Anthony became the first Negro to be elected an officer of the Interfraternity Council at the University of Southern California. Anthony was named secretary of the University's Interfraternity Council. In 1959, at the age of nineteen, he became the nation's youngest editor of a Negro magazine.

Charles Dumas, as a student at the University of Southern California, earned recognition both for his athletic performance and his academic ability. Dumas, a high jumper, was the first person to clear the bar at seven feet. He was selected to be a member of Skull and Dagger, the university's oldest men's honorary group on the campus. (Included in the membership of

Charles Dumas, shown with the University of Southern California track and field coach, was the first man to high jump seven feet.

University Photo
Southern California

University of Indiana News Bureau

Nancy Streets (center) is shown with members of an Indiana University residence hall making preparations for a Mother's Day style show on the Bloomington campus.

Southern California University Photo

Earl Anthony was secretary of the Interfraternity Council, one of the most highly respected and oldest active organizations on the campus of the University of Southern California.

36

Thomas Atkins (right), an honor student, was elected student body president at Indiana University. Shown with Atkins is his election opponent, Mike Dann.

University of Indiana News Bureau

University of North Carolina News Bureau

Julius LaVonne Chambers was editor in chief of the *Law Review,* an official publication of the University of North Carolina Law School, during the 1961-1962 school year.

University of California, Los Angeles

Rafer Johnson, winner of the Decathlon Gold Medal at the 1960 Olympics, served as student body president at the University of California, Los Angeles. He is now engaged in television and motion picture work on the West Coast.

37

this organization are such persons as Walt Disney, the late Frank Lloyd Wright, Episcopal Bishop James A. Pike, and president of the university, Dr. Norman Topping.)

Buford Gibson and Patricia Delker were among thirty-eight students selected to study at the Oak Ridge National Laboratory, a research agency of the United States Atomic Energy Commission. They are studying research techniques in genetics, nuclear science, and organic chemistry.

In addition to the significant roles played by Negroes in American universities and colleges, American Negroes have received Rhodes scholarship awards. *Time* magazine paid tribute to two of these outstanding recipients in its issue of December 28, 1962.

This year not one but two of 23 U. S. Rhodesmen are Negroes. Culled from 544 formidable candidates nominated by colleges across the country, they had to meet Cecil Rhodes's requirement that each of his scholars be "the best man for the world's fight." Few young men have already fought so well:

John E. Wideman, 21, the son of a Pittsburgh waiter, is a senior majoring in English literature at the University of Pennsylvania. Wideman won the campus creative-writing prize, last month got his Phi Beta Kappa key, this year captained Penn's undefeated basketball team. Last week, hours after hurdling the Rhodes selection committee, Captain Wideman led Penn to victory over Vanderbilt, topped his team's scoring with 18 points. His Oxford agenda: language and literature in order to teach college English.

Joseph Stanley Sanders, 20, born in a south Los Angeles slum, is the son of a city garbage-truck driver. Stan's big brother Ed chose one way up—boxing—and died after being knocked out in his ninth pro fight. Stan's way led to top marks at mostly Negro David Starr Jordan High School, thence to a full athletic scholarship at Whittier College, where his size (6 ft. 4 in., 204 lb.) and blinding speed (9.8 sec. for the 100-yd. dash) made him an All-American in small-college football. He also kept A-minus grades in his political science major, was student-body president. Turning down pro football offers, Stan will pursue Oxford's famed "PPE" (philosophy, politics, economics), aims to become a lawyer. He is Whittier's first Rhodes scholar.

EDUCATION AND THE COURTS

The new opportunities in education for all citizens of the United States are due, in part, to the legal efforts of Thurgood Marshall and Dr. James Nabrit. Marshall is now a Federal judge of the United States Second Court of Appeals. He has been one of our nation's outstanding constitutional lawyers. Prior to his present position, he was special counsel for the National Association for the Advancement of Colored People. During his career as a lawyer, Marshall dealt specifically with civil rights cases. He has had as many as 500 cases pending at the same time in various courts. One of his greatest victories was achieved in the case of *Brown v. Board of Education of Topeka*.

Dr. James Nabrit, president of Howard University, is also an outstanding lawyer. His arguments before the Supreme Court in the case of *Bolling v. Sharpe* made history. This case challenged the validity of segregation in the public schools of the District of Columbia, which is under the jurisdiction of the Federal government. The Supreme Court had ruled in *Brown v. Board of*

The Crisis

Thurgood Marshall was the first Negro to be appointed to the United States Court of Appeals. He is probably best known for his work as chief counsel for the NAACP in the field of civil rights.

Education of Topeka that states could no longer maintain racially segregated schools. The Supreme Court decision in *Bolling v. Sharpe* held that racial segregation was likewise unconstitutional in the District of Columbia.

Increasingly, Negroes are becoming aware that in today's world education is important to them. They

Dr. James Nabrit, president of Howard University, is credited with teaching the first civil rights course ever offered at an American school of law.

know that business and industry are asking for men and women with high school and college educations. They know that education builds self-respect for others. They know that education helps them to meet civic responsibilities. They know that acquiring an education provides opportunities to practice effective human relations.

Earning a Living

"A notable development in the United States in recent decades has been the steady improvement in the social and economic status of Negroes."

—JAMES P. MITCHELL
Secretary of Labor

One of the greatest changes now occurring in Negro life evolves from new ways and added opportunities for securing a living. Traditionally, the Negro has been thought of as an unskilled laborer, as a field hand, or as one employed in a service occupation. He still does these things, but it is no longer the whole story. Furthermore, it does not apply to all Negroes. There is growing evidence that this traditional concept is in the process of change.

INCOME AND EMPLOYMENT

One way to ascertain Negro status in the world of employment is to compare his income level with that of Caucasians (Table 1.). The picture becomes still more meaningful when you study the figures dealing with the improvement in nonwhite income according to various income groups (Table 2). The change in the percentages of nonwhites in various occupation groups shown by the figures in Tables 3 and 4 adds still another dimension to the employment picture.

Table 1. Median Wage and Salary Incomes of White and Nonwhite Persons, 1939-60[1]

Year	Male		Female	
	White	Nonwhite	White	Nonwhite
Year-round full-time workers with wage or salary income:				
1939	$1,419	$ 639	$ 863	$ 327
1957	4,950	3,137	3,107	1,866
1958	5,186	3,368	3,225	1,988
1959	5,456	3,339	3,306	2,196
1960	5,662	3,789	3,410	2,372

In all tables and charts "Nonwhites" are 95 percent Negro.

Table 2. Income: All Persons of the Nonwhite Population 14 Years Old and Over with Income[2]

Income	1950	1960
Less than $500	2,048,000	1,944,000
$500 to $999	1,431,000	1,709,000
$1,000 to $1,499	1,000,000	1,061,000
$1,500 to $1,999	781,000	784,000
$2,000 to $2,999	1,046,000	1,395,000
$3,000 to $4,999	383,000	1,776,000
$5,000 and over	43,000	766,000
Median Income	$961	$1,502

Table 3. Distribution of Employed Male Nonwhite Persons by Major Occupations[3]

MAJOR OCCUPATION GROUP	Percent	
	1940	1962
Professional, technical, and kindred workers.....	1.9	4.4
Managers, officials, and proprietors, except farm.	1.6	3.8
Clerical and kindred workers....................	1.2	6.2
Sales workers....................................	.9	1.6
Craftsmen, foremen, and kindred workers.......	4.4	9.0
Operatives, and kindred workers................	12.2	23.7
Laborers, except farm and mine................	20.5	21.9
Service workers, except private household.......	12.4	14.7
Private household workers......................	2.9	.5
Farmers and farm managers....................	21.3	5.4
Farm laborers and foremen....................	19.9	8.6
Occupation not reported.......................	.7	
(Figures rounded to nearest tenth)	99.9	99.8

Table 4. Distribution of Employed Female Nonwhite Persons by Major Occupations[4]

MAJOR OCCUPATION GROUP	Percent 1940	Percent 1962
Professional, technical, and kindred workers.....	4.3	7.4
Managers, officials, and proprietors, except farm.	.8	1.7
Clerical and kindred workers.....................	1.0	10.2
Sales workers...................................	.6	2.2
Craftsmen, foremen, and kindred workers.......	.2	.7
Operatives, and kindred workers.................	6.6	14.6
Laborers, except farm and mine.................	.9	.8
Service workers, except private household.......	10.5	22.5
Private household workers......................	58.0	37.3
Farmers and farm managers....................	3.2	.3
Farm laborers and foremen.....................	12.8	2.4
Occupation not reported.......................	1.1	
(Figures rounded to nearest tenth)	100.0	100.1

The figures in Tables 3 and 4 indicate that several interesting developments took place between 1940 and 1962.

1. The percentage of nonwhite women in clerical and kindred work has increased more than eight times since 1940.
2. The percentage of women working in professional and technical jobs is higher than that of men, although the statistics for men show greater growth.
3. The number of Negroes working in private household service is much lower than in 1940.
4. Private household work continues to be the most frequent unskilled occupation for Negro women.

More than 5.5 million Negroes are employed in American industry—aircraft, automobile, electronics, steel, communications. Of this number, about 50 percent are listed as skilled or semiskilled workers. This is a gain over earlier times, but there remains much to be accomplished. In 1961, the United States Commission on Civil Rights stated:

Although the occupational levels attained by Negroes have risen sharply during the past 20 years, Negro workers are still disproportionately concentrated in the ranks of the unskilled and semiskilled in both private and public employment. They are also disproportionately represented among the unemployed because of their concentration in unskilled and semiskilled jobs, and because Negro workers often have relatively low seniority. These difficulties are due in some degree to present or past discrimination in employment practices, in educational and training opportunities, or both.[5]

In line with efforts now being made to improve working relationships among all people, labor unions are taking action to eliminate racial discrimination from the ranks of trade unions. In a discussion of this topic, which appeared in the November 25, 1962, issue of the *Press-Enterprise* of Riverside, California, Burnell Phillips, a labor union official, stated that an official of the AFL-CIO Civil Rights Committee had notified the Vice-President of the United States that "87 national and international unions representing some nine million members have volunteered to sign fair practice pledges." These pledges, Phillips wrote, "are similar to the 'plans for progress' signed earlier by a number of industrial firms, including the nation's biggest defense contractors, aimed at insuring fair employment practices." These fair practices pledges will commit each union to:

1. Accept all eligible applicants for membership, without regard to race, creed, color, or national origin.
2. Seek management agreement on non-discrimination practices in all conditions of employment, including hiring, tenure, work assignments, training programs, promotions, transfers, and use of employee facilities.

3. Refuse to charter any local union on a segregated basis and to end segregation in any locals where it now exists.

4. Seek management agreement on clauses guaranteeing non-discrimination in joint apprenticeship programs and insuring their full and effective administration.[6]

This program, a voluntary one for AFL-CIO affiliates, may be of real significance in the whole field of civil rights, and specifically in the area of securing a living. Actually, success of the program will depend on the extent to which local unions honor the pledges of their national organizations.

GOVERNMENT EMPLOYMENT

The change in employment opportunities for Negroes is dramatically illustrated by the number of nonwhites employed by the Federal, state, and local governments. Figures released by the Department of Labor show that the number of nonwhites employed by all levels of government increased from 214,000 in 1940 to about 1,000,000 in 1962. In 1940, nonwhites comprised 5.6 percent of the government work force. By 1962, this figure had increased to 12.1 percent.[7] A Federal employment study made in June, 1963, revealed that 301,889 Negroes were employed by the Federal government. This figure represented 13.1 percent of the 2,298,808 Federal jobs.

Approximately 2,000,000 Federal employees are under civil service. Of this number about 240,000, or more than 12 percent, are nonwhite. Many types of civil service careers are open to Negroes. These include jobs as postal clerks and carriers, accountants, educators, investigators, FBI workers, and administrative assistants in such Federal agencies as the Internal Revenue Service or the United States Housing and Home Finance Agency.

NEGROES AS GOVERNMENT ADMINISTRATORS

DR. ROBERT WEAVER

The United States Housing and Home Finance Agency (HHFA) is of major importance to many persons interested in housing. The head of this agency is Dr. Robert Clifton Weaver, a Negro. Dr. Weaver is responsible, under the President, for administering the Federal government's principal programs for better housing and better communities. The HHFA consists of the Office of the Administrator and five constituents.

United States Official Photo

Robert C. Weaver is shown as he testified before a Senate committee prior to his confirmation as United States Housing Administrator.

Each constituent agency has its own area of responsibility in a broad, coordinated program which includes aid to low-rent public housing, multi-family projects, mortgage insurance for individual homes, grants and loans for slum clearance and urban renewal, and many related activities. The annual budget of the agency is about four billion dollars.

Dr. Weaver's interest in housing and urban problems began years before his appointment as Housing Administrator. During the administration of Franklin D. Roosevelt, Dr. Weaver served as an adviser on Negro affairs in the Department of the Interior, and he was active in the development of the housing activities for which he is now responsible. Following his departure from government service in 1944, Dr. Weaver was executive director of the Mayor's Committee on Race Relations in Chicago, and later served the state of New York as deputy commissioner of housing and as administrator of the Housing Rent Commission. When appointed to his present post, he was vice-chairman of the Housing and Re-development Board of the City of New York. Dr. Weaver, who earned a Ph.D. from Harvard, was the first Negro to hold a cabinet-rank post in state government.

DR. RALPH BUNCHE

The name of Dr. Ralph Bunche must be included in any discussion of those who have made significant contributions in the fields of government and diplomacy. After receiving a Ph.D. in political science from Harvard in 1934, Dr. Bunche did post-doctoral work in London and South Africa. He is considered an authority on colonialism.

During World War II, Dr. Bunche was assigned to the Office of Strategic Services. His research on colonial and African affairs was of vital importance to the Allies in helping them plan the defense of these geographical areas.

Following World War II, Dr. Bunche was appointed by the State Department to help formulate the Charter of the United Nations. When the United Nations became a reality, Dr. Bunche was made a member of its staff. Because of his contributions, he assumed various high-level assignments in the United Nations organization.

One of Dr. Bunche's best known assignments was that of acting mediator to help bring about an armistice in the war in Palestine between Israel and the Arab League. Although the task of bringing peace between these warring nations was not an easy one, Dr. Bunche was successful. After forty-one days of negotiating, an

United Nations

This scene was photographed during the negotiations to end fighting between Egypt and Israel in 1949. Dr. Ralph Bunche, chairman of the UN mission and chief moderator, is seated third from the left.

49

armistice was signed. In recognition of his successful efforts in bringing about this armistice, Dr. Bunche received the 1950 Nobel Peace Prize.

CARL T. ROWAN

One of the highest-ranking Negro officials in the Federal government is Carl T. Rowan, Director of the United States Information Agency (USIA). The purpose of this Agency is to help create an understanding abroad of American foreign policies. The USIA sponsors the Voice of America radio broadcasts which provide truthful news for people living in totalitarian societies. It maintains libraries and information centers in many nations.

U. S. Information Agency

Carl Rowan, outstanding journalist and former Ambassador to Finland, was appointed Director of the United States Information Agency by President Johnson in 1964. Rowan thus became the first Negro to serve on the National Security Council.

The Director of the USIA advises the President on the climate of opinion in foreign countries and also meets with the National Security Council. Mr. Rowan was the first Negro to attend meetings of this Council. Prior to his appointment as USIA Director in January, 1964, Mr. Rowan was Ambassador to Finland, a post to which President Kennedy appointed him in 1963. He began his government work in 1961 when he was appointed Deputy Assistant Secretary of State for Public Affairs.

Mr. Rowan earned a master's degree in journalism from the University of Minnesota. He worked for thirteen years as a reporter for the *Minneapolis Tribune,* and won several awards for his excellent news stories. He also is the author of four books.

THE FOREIGN SERVICE

A vital area in which the American Negro is serving is with the United States Department of State, which was established in 1789. Secretary of State was the first Cabinet post created by Congress and is the highest-ranking Cabinet position. The Secretary of State is a direct link between the President of the United States and foreign governments.

One of the functions of the Department of State is to supervise the assignments of the Foreign Service—the ambassadors, ministers, and consular officers. There are about twenty Negro Foreign Service officers, and about forty more are serving on the Foreign Service staff. Among those serving in the Foreign Service are Clifford Wharton and Mercer Cook, ambassadors to Norway and Niger respectively; David Bolen, economic officer for the United States in Ghana; Charles Hanson, labor officer, Trinidad; Archie Samuel, administrative officer,

Pakistan; James Parker, consular officer, Spain; Clinton Knox, deputy director of political affairs, Paris; and Leslie Polk, head of the economic section of the American Embassy, Damascus, Syria. These men are university graduates with excellent qualifications for the services they perform. Some of them hold doctorate degrees, have a knowledge of several foreign languages, and are experienced in government both at home and abroad.

The work of Foreign Service officers is important to our country. They work closely with leaders in other countries. The impressions made by Foreign Service representatives on the leaders of other countries affects the decisions of those leaders as they relate to the United States.

Positions with the United States Department of State and in the Foreign Service are open to all qualified persons. Officers of the Foreign Service have a salary range of $7,000 to $20,000, with an expense allowance for career ambassadors.

One of the newer agencies in which qualified persons may serve is the Peace Corps. Negro members of the Peace Corps' Advisory Council include Harry Belafonte, singer; Dr. Benjamin Mays, president of Morehouse College; and Dr. Albert Dent, president of Dillard University. There are many other Negroes serving in the Peace Corps overseas. Howard University has the distinction of being one of the universities selected to train persons entering the Peace Corps.

SERVICE IN OTHER BRANCHES OF GOVERNMENT

Negroes are active in many different fields of government work. Some of these have been noted. In addition, five Negroes are serving as congressmen. There are Negroes in twenty-three of our state legislatures. They serve at all levels of the judiciary, as city attorneys, on voting registration boards, on school boards, as city councilmen, and as postmasters.

Although we have discussed some of the important positions in government occupied by Negroes, it should not be assumed that all Negroes serving in government are employed in high-ranking positions. Many are working for the government as secretaries, clerks, repairmen, guards, custodians, and other types of work covering a wide range of skilled and unskilled work.

PRESIDENTIAL ORDER ENDS DISCRIMINATION IN DEFENSE INDUSTRIES

Positions in government for Negroes began to develop on a major scale in 1941 when President Roosevelt issued his now famous Executive Order 8802. This statement related to fair employment practices in our national defense programs. It was designed to eliminate discrimination against persons of any race, creed, color, or national origin who sought work in defense industry. Executive Order 8802 stated:

Whereas it is the policy of the United States to encourage full participation in the national defense program by all citizens of the United States, regardless of race, creed, color, or national origin, in the firm belief that the democratic way of life within the nation can be defended successfully only with the help and support of all groups within its borders; and

Whereas there is evidence that available and needed workers have been barred from employment in industries engaged in defense production solely because of considerations of race, creed, color, or national origin, to the detriment of workers' morale and of national unity;

Now, Therefore, by virtue of the authority vested in me by the Constitution and the statutes, and as a prerequisite to the successful conduct of our national defense production effort, I do hereby reaffirm the policy of the United States that there shall be no discrimination in the employment of workers in defense industries or government because of race, creed, color, or national origin, and I do hereby declare that it is the duty of employers and of labor organizations, in furtherance of said policy and of this order, to provide for the full and equitable participation of all workers in defense industries, without discrimination because of race, creed, color, or national origin:

And it is hereby ordered as follows:

1. All departments and agencies of the Government of the United States concerned with vocational training programs for defense production shall take special measures appropriate to assure that such programs are administered without discrimination because of race, creed, color, or national origin;

2. All contracting agencies of the Government of the United States shall include in all defense contracts hereafter negotiated by them a provision obligating the contractor not to discriminate against any worker because of race, creed, color, or national origin;

3. There is established in the Office of Production Management a Committee on Fair Employment Practice, which shall consist of a chairman and four other members to be appointed by the President. The Chairman and members of the Committee shall serve as such without compensation, but shall be entitled to actual and neces-

sary transportation, subsistence and other expense incidental to performance of their duties. The Committee shall receive and investigate complaints of discrimination in violation of the provisions of this order and shall take appropriate steps to redress grievances which it finds to be valid. The Committee shall also recommend to the several departments and agencies of the Government of the United States and to the President all measures which may be deemed by it necessary or proper to effectuate the provisions of this order.[8]

FAIR EMPLOYMENT PRACTICE LAWS

This Executive Order set a precedent for what we now know as "fair employment practices" which have been established by many states in our nation. Fair employment practice laws are based upon the idea that equal employment opportunities should be given to all citizens. The following release by the United States Department of Labor comments on these laws:

By July 1962, 20 States, having 60 percent of the U.S. population and nearly 40 percent of the Nation's Negro population, had passed enforceable fair employment practice laws designed to end discrimination in private employment. Two other states, Indiana and Idaho, had fair employment practice laws, but without enforcement provisions. Many of the State fair employment practice commissions are charged with enforcing nondiscrimination regulations in public accommodation, housing, or education as well as in employment.

As a rule, the State law creates a commission having enforcement power. In practice, however, the commissions proceed largely through public education, following their investigation of a complaint with an attempt to persuade the offender to end the practice complained of. If necessary, a formal hearing can be held. After a hearing the commission may issue an order, and this order may be enforced if necessary through the courts. Few cases in any State, however, reach the stage of formal hearing, and very few reach the courts. The commissions depend largely on education and conciliation; they claim to have achieved good results by these means.[9]

BUSINESS

One of the most noteworthy changes involving the economic life of Negroes is the increasing numbers of business enterprises which they now own and operate. Insurance, real estate, publishing, and cosmetics are among the most important fields in which Negroes have become established. It is interesting to note that the first Negro woman to become a millionaire obtained her wealth from cosmetics. Insurance and real estate rank high as sources of income for many of America's richest Negroes.

The field of insurance offers an excellent example of the success achieved by Negroes in the business community. Negroes now own and operate more than sixty-five insurance companies with over 250 million dollars of insurance in force. Among the most successful of the insurance companies owned by Negroes is the Universal Life Insurance Company of Memphis, Tennessee. This company employs more than 700 persons and has assets in excess of 22 million dollars. In 1962, the members of the National Insurance Association paid tribute to the success of Negroes in this field by electing George Beavers, Jr., a Negro, as their president.

Another area of business in which Negroes have made substantial progress is banking. Despite the fact that banks owned by Negroes are comparatively new, there are at least fourteen such banks with combined resources of more than 40 million dollars.

Virtually all reports on Negro business activity indicate that Negroes have not given much emphasis to small business firms as a means of securing a living. For the most part, Negroes have found it difficult to secure the capital and credit necessary to venture into the highly competitive world of small business. But as educational and business opportunities increase, the Negro will no doubt find this area profitable.

EDUCATION

Negroes have been active as teachers for many years. Today they are obtaining more positions in all schools, including colleges and universities. The percentage of Negro teachers in the public schools of California increased from less than 1 percent in 1940 to about 4 percent in 1962. The significance of these figures is not the actual numbers involved but rather in the fact that they show an increase, a trend, and evolving status that augurs well for the future.

ADVERTISING

The Negro is finding a new source of income in the field of merchandising. Both female and male models are now being employed to advertise various kinds of products ranging from clothing to household appliances. Negroes are shown on television advertising products which have a nationwide distribution. They are shown in magazines with nationwide circulation. Gains have also been made in the creative field of commercial advertising. A well-known New York firm employs a

Negro, Georg Olden, as a graphic arts designer. In this position, he designs and directs television commercials for some of the nation's leading firms.

ARMED FORCES

The nation's armed forces offer many career possibilities for all persons. Today all people can proceed with increased confidence that they will be able to earn positions of leadership if they are qualified and put forth their best efforts.

More than 200,000 Negroes are serving in the armed forces, and many are taking advantage of the career possibilities open to them. It is significant that some 5,000 of them are now serving as commissioned or warrant officers.

SCIENCE

An increasing number of American Negroes are finding careers in science. Although science is not a new career area for them, they are finding new opportunities and incentives in the needs of our Space Age, in our changing social structure, and in the need to utilize all of America's human resources.

Negroes have been involved in some areas of science for many years. For example, one Negro received a Ph.D. degree in physics in 1876, and another received a Ph.D. in biology in 1889. It was not until 1925, however, that Elbert Cox became the first Negro to receive a Ph.D. degree in mathematics. Since that time, other Negroes have attained a height of scholastic recognition and scientific achievement that has enabled them to be listed among America's men of science.

Over the years, Negroes have made numerous important contributions to the development of American science and industry. A brief look at some of the outstanding Negro contributors will give you some idea of the role played by Negroes in bringing American science and industry to its present high state.

Jan Matzeliger developed a new process in shoe manufacturing. In the 1870s, Matzeliger invented a device called a "lasting machine." This machine introduced a revolutionary way of holding a shoe on its form until the leather was attached and the nails were driven into place around the sole. Thus, the making of a shoe was completed in one process. This machine saved many hours of hand work previously done by the shoe cobbler. This invention contributed materially to greater shoe production during America's industrial expansion and to the development of the shoe industry throughout the nation.

Elijah McCoy invented an oil cup to lubricate machine parts that are in motion. Success in keeping the various moving parts of machinery in operation depends upon the use of lubricants. You may observe that many things which you and your parents own, a bicycle, an automobile, or a sewing machine, require regular lubrication for smooth operation of the moving metal parts. Before the discovery of oil, a greasy substance such as pork was used for lubricating industrial machinery. As a result, constant attention was required to keep the machinery in operation. In 1872, Elijah McCoy invented an oil cup that mechanically supplied oil and grease to machinery and engines. Although the oil and grease supply had to be replenished periodically, machinery could operate for days and even weeks with little or no attention to lubrication. This invention helped to speed production because it kept machines operating at full capacity. In addition to the oil cup, McCoy had numerous other inventions to his credit. Altogether he registered nearly sixty patents. His inventions and discoveries have been put to use in factories, on steamships, and in locomotives.

According to Admiral Peary, Matthew Henson was a "co-discoverer" of the North Pole. Firsthand information about the North Pole, the object of an intensive search by many nations, and the Arctic regions sur-

MATTHEW ALEXANDER HENSON
CO-DISCOVERER OF THE NORTH POLE
WITH
ADMIRAL ROBERT EDWIN PEARY
APRIL 6, 1909
BORN AUGUST 8, 1866   DIED MARCH 9, 1955

SON OF MARYLAND
EXEMPLIFICATION OF COURAGE, FORTITUDE AND PATRIOTISM,
WHOSE VALIANT DEEDS OF NOBLE DEVOTION
UNDER THE COMMAND OF ADMIRAL ROBERT EDWIN PEARY

State of Maryland

Matthew Henson received many honors for his contributions to science. This memorial tablet is in the State House, Annapolis, Maryland.

rounding it was made available as the result of expeditions by Peary and Henson. In recognition of his contributions, Henson was awarded an honorary degree in science and the Congressional Medal of Honor. In addition, provisions were made for the establishment of permanent memorials to Mr. Henson. One was placed in the State House at Annapolis, Maryland, and a small replica of the same was placed on the campus of the Pomonkey High School, near Indian Head, Maryland.

George Washington Carver discovered ways to synthesize more than three hundred products from the peanut. The synthesized products created as a result of Dr. Carver's research include five kinds of breakfast foods, ten kinds of milk, cooking oils, dyes, stains, linoleum, inks, cheese, and peanut butter.

As a result of George Washington Carver's work, the United Peanut Association of America asked Dr. Carver, in 1921, to appear before the Ways and Means Committee of the House of Representatives in support of a request for economic aid from the Federal government. Following Dr. Carver's testimony, aid was granted in the form of a protective duty against foreign peanut trade coming into this country.

In addition to his work with the peanut, Dr. Carver has made many other important contributions to our economy. From the sweet potato, he synthesized chocolates, caramels, library paste, instant coffee, rope, and molasses. He demonstrated to farmers how to rotate their crops for better production. He showed how a whole rainbow of dye colors could be made from the rich Alabama clay.

George Washington Carver, through research and practical experience, has contributed more than any other single American to the science of chemurgy, the science of chemically converting farm and forest products for industrial uses. His ideas and formulas for utilizing farm crops in industry are considered the foundation of chemurgy. Working in his laboratory at Tuskegee Institute in Alabama (1896-1943), George Washington Carver developed formulas in agricultural chemistry that have benefited all mankind.

Dr. Carver spent most of his life at Tuskegee carrying on research, and established a research foundation in agricultural chemistry with his own life savings. In spite of all his contributions to agricultural chemistry, this humble person refused to apply for a patent on any of his discoveries. He said, "God gave them to me. Why should I claim to own them?"

In tribute to this great scientist, President Truman proclaimed a George Washington Carver Day in 1946. A portion of the President's proclamation is given below:

> Whereas it is fitting that we honor the memory of George Washington Carver, who contributed to the expansion of the agricultural economy of the nation through his diligent research as an agricultural chemist . . . I do hereby call upon the officials of the government to have the flag of the United States displayed on all government buildings on January 5, 1946, in commemoration of the achievements of George Washington Carver.[10]

John W. Blanton contributed to America's first jet-propelled aircraft. During World War II, John W. Blanton, research engineer in thermodynamics, assisted in the design of production models of the P-59 Airacomet, the first jet-propelled airplane in America. Today, Blanton is nationally known in the field of guided missiles.

Percy Julian did important research in many areas of science. It was reported that seventy years of research with the drug physostigmine had not produced the answer to its chemical make-up in its natural form. Neither had it been determined why this drug, when used externally, caused the pupil of the eye to contract. The answer was finally discovered in 1935 by Percy Julian, an organic chemist, while he was studying for his doctorate degree at the University of Vienna. His research findings dealing with the structure and synthesizing of physostigmine, a drug used for the treatment of glaucoma (hardening of the eyeball), was only one of his important contributions in the field of science.

Percy Julian graduated from DePauw University. He was both a member of Phi Beta Kappa and the valedictorian of his class. While at DePauw, Dr. Julian worked as a waiter in a fraternity house. He used the attic for his sleeping quarters. Dr. Julian also attended Harvard University and later studied in Vienna. He was named "Man of the Year" in greater Chicago by one of that city's newspapers.

Dr. Julian and his co-workers have registered more than forty patents. A few of these relate to making cold-water paints, preparing plastic materials, and isolating sterol from soy bean oil. Dr. Julian has discovered a substance to relieve the pain of arthritis. His discovery of a better means of extinguishing oil and grease fires saved many lives aboard American ships during World War II. He has contributed many important scientific articles to chemical journals and accounts of his discoveries have been translated into several languages.

Lloyd Hall made significant contributions to the food industry. Lloyd Hall, a food chemist, has registered more than eighty patents in Canada and Great Britain as well as the United States. He serves as a consultant to many major companies in the food industry. His services are concerned with problems of how to keep America's food supply pure, sanitary, and pleasing to the taste.

MEDICINE

The Negro is making great strides in the field of medicine and is finding more career opportunities opening to him. Medical schools and hospitals now are less concerned about the ethnic background of academically qualified applicants. They are accepting increasing numbers of qualified Negro applicants. Today nearly one hundred Negroes are listed among the Fellows of the American College of Surgeons.

Many advances have been made and are being made through medical research by Negroes studying in their special fields. Dr. Theodore Lawless, one of the pioneers in the field of dermatology (diseases of the skin), and Dr. Harold Pierce are nationally known dermatologists. Dr. Pierce is given credit for developing a treatment to deal more effectively with scars resulting from acne.

Dr. Charles R. Drew long will be remembered for his experimental work in the field of blood chemistry and blood transfusions. Dr. Drew was the first doctor to use successfully blood plasma for emergency transfusions. Others had considered the idea but it was Dr. Drew who really put it to work.

In the early stages of his research, Dr. Drew noted that both stored blood and fresh blood often caused headaches in patients receiving transfusions. Furthermore, it was noted that patients receiving such transfusions developed chills or a fever. Then too, there was the problem of obtaining the right type of blood for a patient's specific needs. Often the right type of blood was

Dr. Charles Drew's research in the uses of blood and blood plasma was a major factor in the establishment of modern blood banks.

not immediately available and storing blood had its problems. Would plasma do the job? Dr. Drew knew that it contained all of the substances of whole blood except the red cells. Since it seemed to be the red cell that caused much of the difficulty in using whole blood, Dr. Drew concluded that plasma was the answer.

It is impossible to say how many lives have been saved by Dr. Drew's work. His discovery was especially valuable during World War II when time for transfusions was short, and a battlefield patient couldn't wait until a blood of his type was obtained. It is estimated that of all the wounded men given blood plasma during World War II, 96 out of every 100 recovered.[11]

Dentistry is a branch of medicine that is attracting an increasing number of Negroes. Some of them are going on to postgraduate work to become specialists in such fields as orthodontics, periodontics, and oral surgery. Today there are Negro specialists licensed by state boards of dental examiners or certified by American specialty boards. As in the case of doctors, the number of dentists is far too small for the need. It is of interest to note that the first dental school established by one of our major universities was founded at Harvard in 1867. Six young men were accepted for the first class. One was a Negro.

NURSING

The care of the sick is a career that requires much work and a high degree of dedication. Today a qualified Negro girl can choose almost any school in which to take her nurse's training. As a nurse she will find that one of the goals of the American Nurses Association (ANA) is to provide equal rights and opportunities for all persons. By 1961, integration had taken place in 53 of the 54 constituent units of the ANA.

ARCHITECTURE

American Negroes have found employment and careers in architecture. One of the outstanding persons in this field is Paul R. Williams, who has won national recognition. Mr. Williams has designed homes ranging from modest dwellings to palatial residences. He has been employed often as the chief architect or as a consultant for city and commercial building projects such as churches, auditoriums, schools, and hotels. His design for the Music Corporation of America Building in Beverly Hills, California, brought him an award from the American Institute of Architects for designing "one of the most beautiful buildings in southern California." In 1951, Williams was selected to design a shrine for the late Al Jolson.

Mr. Williams believes that homes should be designed around an individual's personality and around the way a person lives. Commercial structures, according to Williams, should be planned according to the purpose of the business they house. As early as 1940, Williams predicted that the trend of architecture would be toward a simplification of buildings, and that much attention would be given to good proportion and to the use of color. Today, the accuracy of that prediction is evident in the design of ultra-modern buildings throughout the United States.

ATHLETICS

The progress of the American Negro is nowhere better illustrated than in high school, college, and professional sports. While Negroes have their famous names in sports, the significant fact is not that a few persons are stars but, rather, that thousands are playing because they have had an equal chance to make the team. Athletics has become a career area for many Negroes. More important, it has become a means of attending a college or university in order to obtain an education.

The names of outstanding university and professional athletes may change from year to year, but the name of Jackie Robinson long will be remembered. The first Negro to play on an organized Major League baseball team (1947), Robinson had his problems as well as his achievements. That he was able to succeed, both in baseball and in human relations, has meant an "open door," sooner than expected, for Negroes to become a part of organized, professional sports. Current Negro stars such as Willie Mays, Ernie Banks, and Hank Aaron have earned their own place in organized baseball, but Robinson was the first Negro selected. Robinson was elected recently to baseball's Hall of Fame.

Whether it is in baseball, basketball, football, golf, or other organized sports, the American Negro is not only experiencing a high degree of success, but he is also becoming better known and better understood because of his athletic activities. Individually or as a member of a team, he performs daily before large audiences. Television brings him into the homes of additional millions of Americans.

MUSIC

The Negro has provided a rich cultural heritage for America. The unique and original styles of music known as Negro spirituals and modern jazz have been contributions of lasting quality and sources of income for many persons in all the art forms. Negro spirituals and the life of the Negro have served as themes for many outstanding musical works by American composers and artists such as Paul Whiteman, George Gershwin, and Stephen Foster. Negro spirituals and folk songs are as popular today as they were when this music first appeared on the American scene.

America's first native music is credited to the Negro. Actually, America's spiritual music is a product of Negro life. It was the early families, working and living on the plantations, who made up songs of happiness, sorrow, love, and hope for a better life. These unwritten songs were sung to children by their elders and thus were passed on from generation to generation. Finally, they were called the folk songs of the Negro. It was not until 1867 that this rich source of music was discovered for its unique contribution and was made available in printed form. This momentous task was accomplished by William Allen. He published *Slave Songs of the United States,* a transcribed collection of the melodies he had heard. Today, these songs are universally referred to as Negro spirituals. In their melodic form, it was the Fisk (University) Jubilee Singers who interpreted the spirituals. This group carried the spirituals throughout the United States and Europe. As a result, the spirituals won universal acceptance and recognition. An example of this acceptance is to be found in the thematic material for symphonic music composed in 1894 by Anton Dvorák. He chose the spirituals, along with other folk themes, to represent the American mood in his world-famous symphony, *From the New World.* The contribution made by the spirituals is regarded as one of the most valuable elements in American music as we know it today. You may hear many of these spirituals sung or played by the world's outstanding musicians. Sometimes you may hear them arranged as sacred or classical music. On other occasions, you may hear them as jazz music.

Jazz emerged in the last half of the 19th century as a distinctly American form of music. The American Negro is primarily responsible for developing jazz from African and European rhythms. New Orleans was the jazz center until touring musicians like Joseph "King" Oliver and Louis Armstrong made it popular throughout the nation. At the same time, vocal blues, another jazz form, became popular. W. C. Handy and his "St. Louis Blues" set the style for the leading singers Bessie Smith and Ma Rainey. Two other great musicians were "Jelly Roll" Morton and Freddie Kepard.

From the 1920s to the 1960s, jazz styles changed from traditional to swing, bebop, and finally "cool" jazz. Lester Young, John "Dizzy" Gillespie, Charlie Parker, Miles Davis, and Count Basie contributed to the various changes. Vocal styles changed as well, with the sounds of Ella Fitzgerald, Billie Holiday, and Sarah Vaughan. Although American in origin, jazz is popular throughout the world.

Marian Anderson is one of America's most renowned concert artists. The celebrated symphony conductor, Arturo Toscanini, after hearing Miss Anderson sing, said, "What I have heard today one is privileged to hear only once in a hundred years." Miss Anderson has appeared in concert throughout the United States, in Europe, in Africa, and in Asia. Wherever she sings, Miss Anderson always includes a selection of Negro spirituals.

In 1961, Miss Anderson was named as one of the world's "ten most-admired women" by an American Institute of Public Opinion poll, conducted by George Gallup. Other names on the list included Mrs. Eleanor Roosevelt, Queen Elizabeth, Mme. Chiang Kai-shek, and Mrs. John F. Kennedy.

The voice of Leontyne Price has contributed to the pleasure and musical appreciation of many opera audiences in this country and abroad. Miss Price sang the lead role in *Tosca* when she made her television debut in 1955. Following this triumphant performance, she made her grand opera stage debut in 1957 at San Francisco. *Mademoiselle* magazine selected Miss Price as one of the "ten outstanding women" in 1955. A long-time ambition was realized on January 27, 1961, when Miss Price appeared on the stage of the Metropolitan Opera House in New York City. For Miss Price, "singing is the only important thing."

In one of her appearances at the Metropolitan Opera House, Miss Leontyne Price sang the role of Cio-Cio-San in *Madame Butterfly*.

American Negroes have appeared in operatic roles since 1872 outside the United States. It has been only within the past thirty years, however, that they have participated in America. In 1936, for example, Miss Anderson became the first Negro to appear in concert at the Metropolitan Opera House. In 1955, Miss Price became the first to appear in a lead role in a major opera in this country.

Probably no one person in the history of modern jazz classics has exerted a stronger influence upon its development than Duke Ellington, composer and pianist. He is a pioneer contributor to the jazz classics. His compositions embody the basic musical qualities of harmony, melody, form, and rhythm. His style has set basic patterns for modern jazz. In addition, Duke Ellington has contributed to the field of symphonic jazz, and many of his suites have been performed by leading musicians of our day. He has composed background music for dramatic plays on stage, television, and radio. Altogether, Duke Ellington has contributed a rich heritage of compositions in both popular and semi-classical music. Among his best known compositions are "Mood Indigo," "Solitude," and "Sophisticated Lady."

Some Negroes have become wealthy as a result of their work in music. Many others have earned a good living, and still others have not been quite so successful. Whatever the case may be, the American Negro long has found in music not only an area of interest but also an area in which his talents are rewarded.

JOB OPPORTUNITIES INCREASE
AS NEGRO POPULATION SHIFTS

In order to reflect on the changing position of the Negro at work, it is necessary to understand that he is

Table 5. Population of United States, by Race: 1960[12]
(In thousands, rounded)

States	Whites	Negroes	Percent
United States	158,832	18,872	10.5
Alabama	2,284	980	30.0
Alaska	175	7	3.0
Arizona	1,170	43	3.3
Arkansas	1,396	389	21.8
California	14,455	884	5.6
Colorado	1,701	40	2.3
Connecticut	2,424	107	4.2
Delaware	384	61	13.6
Dist. of Columbia	345	412	53.9
Florida	4,064	880	17.8
Georgia	2,817	1,123	28.5
Hawaii	202	5	0.8
Idaho	657	2	0.2
Illinois	9,010	1,037	10.3
Indiana	4,389	269	5.8
Iowa	2,729	25	0.9
Kansas	2,079	91	4.2
Kentucky	2,820	216	7.1
Louisiana	2,212	1,039	31.9
Maine	963	3	0.3
Maryland	2,574	518	16.7
Massachusetts	5,023	112	2.2
Michigan	7,086	718	9.2
Minnesota	3,372	22	0.7
Mississippi	1,258	916	42.0
Missouri	3,923	391	9.0
Montana	651	1	0.2
Nebraska	1,375	29	2.1
Nevada	263	13	4.7
New Hampshire	604	2	0.3
New Jersey	5,539	515	8.5
New Mexico	876	17	1.8
New York	15,287	1,418	8.4
North Carolina	3,399	1,116	24.5
North Dakota	620	1	0.1
Ohio	8,910	786	8.1
Oklahoma	2,108	153	6.6
Oregon	1,732	18	1.0
Pennsylvania	10,454	853	7.5
Rhode Island	839	18	2.1
South Carolina	1,551	829	34.8
South Dakota	653	1	0.2
Tennessee	2,978	587	16.5
Texas	8,375	1,187	12.4
Utah	874	4	0.5
Vermont	389	1	0.1
Virginia	3,142	816	20.6
Washington	2,752	49	1.7
West Virginia	1,770	89	4.8
Wisconsin	3,859	75	1.9
Wyoming	323	2	0.7

no longer confined to the rural and agricultural South. Before 1900, about 75 percent of the nation's Negroes lived in rural areas, particularly of the South. But by 1960, only 28 percent of the Negro population was rural. The remainder was divided between Southern cities and Northern or Western cities. Some of the states with the largest increases in Negro population are New York, California, Illinois, Florida, Michigan, Ohio, Pennsylvania, Texas, and New Jersey. In the last ten years 1.5 million Negroes have moved from the South to the North and West. Table 5 shows the white and nonwhite population of all states in 1960.

The movement of the Negro into many regions of our country has provided new job opportunities for him because of varied types of work in different geographical locations. World War II was another force that affected the Negro and his opportunities for a career. During the war, all of America's manpower was mobilized to achieve victory. In addition, education and the "equal opportunity" position taken by the Federal government and many state governments helped improve the job opportunities for Negroes. The trained Negro is finding it easier to secure employment than ever before. Some evidence of this may be seen from an article, "Recruiting Negroes," which appeared in *The Wall Street Journal* on August 6, 1962. The article notes that more business representatives are now visiting Negroes about to graduate from college. The article stated:

> The corporate recruiter is beating a path to institutes of higher learning he's long passed up—Negro colleges . . .
>
> Howard University, a leading Negro school in Washington, D. C., received more than 200 visits from industry

and government job recruiters this year. This was more than three times the number of visits in 1961 . . .

Negro students are beginning to show more willingness to prepare for jobs they once never considered for fear of being rebuffed.

All this is only part of the growing evidence that the American Negro is both searching for and finding new and better ways to earn a living—a living characterized by higher status, greater service, added responsibility, and increased income.

While the Negro is making progress in the working world, he cannot be satisfied with his present-day achievements. This is evident from the fact that although he accounts for one in ten workers, he also accounts for about two in ten of the unemployed. The high rate of Negro unemployment is due chiefly to discrimination and the large number of unskilled workers.

As the Negro makes decisions about his career, more than ever before he must consider the working implications of automation. Because of automation, fewer unskilled laborers are needed. This means that more persons must prepare themselves for work involving skilled technical and professional accomplishments. A question for the future might well be, "Will there be enough qualified Negroes to take advantage of the opportunities available to them?"

Housing, Transportation, and Public Accommodations

New York City has the largest Negro population of any city in the United States, about 1.1 million persons. Following New York are Chicago, Philadelphia, Detroit, Washington, Los Angeles, and Baltimore. The population of Washington, D.C., is about 54 percent Negro. Approximately 33 percent of the populations of Atlanta, New Orleans, Memphis, and Baltimore are Negro. Homes for Negroes are needed, not only in these large cities but, of course, wherever they live.

OBTAINING A HOME

One of the most serious problems facing Negro families is concerned with housing. The author of a recent and thorough study on this subject, Luigi Laurenti, states that Negroes are faced with restrictions that white people do not have:

> They will find their search for a home held inside certain geographical bounds because (1) the community may, for a complex of reasons, resist their moving into certain neighborhoods; (2) individual white property

owners . . . may refuse to sell to them; (3) real estate brokers and agents, motivated by a combination of community pressure, a real estate code of ethics, instructions of sellers, and personal feelings, may direct them into limited areas "approved" for nonwhite residence; and (4) real estate loans may be unavailable—or available only on terms less favorable than those for white borrowers. That Negro and other nonwhite customers do not have access to all the houses for sale in their local community is a widely recognized and accepted fact of life.[1]

Reasons given for restricting certain racial groups to housing in limited areas of a community include the idea that when Negroes or members of other nonwhite groups enter a white housing area, property values decline. Upon investigating this idea and reviewing the research of others, Laurenti concluded that property values do not necessarily decline when Negroes obtain housing in a previously all-white area. In fact, property values may even rise.[2]

Another idea often heard is that a Negro doesn't keep his property in good condition. Laurenti disputes this idea. He writes, "Evidence that is available strongly suggests that nonwhites who are buying homes in formerly white neighborhoods are 'keeping up with the Joneses' in taking care of their property."[3]

While prejudice cannot be ignored as a force restricting Negro opportunities to purchase homes, it is not the only force of significance. Others include degree of wealth, type of career, and historical background.

One of the ways Negroes are excluded from the right to obtain the homes they want and can afford in a community involves what are called "race-restrictive covenants." These are agreements among homeowners not to sell to persons of certain racial or religious backgrounds. Such agreements have no legal status. The Supreme Court has ruled that race-restrictive covenants are not enforceable in our courts.

Any discussion of housing must emphasize the inadequate housing conditions for those Negroes who live in low income areas of our large cities. Conditions in these areas are characterized by over-crowding; lack of privacy; a minimum of modern facilities such as plumbing, ventilation, and good lighting; the lack of healthy recreational facilities; and the difficulty of creating an aesthetic environment. Because of this, thousands of children and teenage persons in these low income areas are experiencing daily living conditions that encourage undesirable behavior. In 1961, the United States Commission on Civil Rights stated:

> Denial of equal housing opportunity means essentially the deliberate exclusion of many minority group members from a large part of the housing market and to a large extent confinement in deteriorating ghettos. It involves more than poverty and slums, for it extends to the denial of a fundamental part of freedom: choice in an open competitive market. This is a strange phenomenon in a nation that cherishes individual freedom.[4]

The Commission further notes:

> Housing . . . seems to be the one commodity in the American market that is not freely available on equal terms to everyone who can afford to pay.[5]

The Federal government has enacted legislation designed to help the Negro deal on an equal basis with white persons in acquiring a home. If, for example, the Federal government helps to finance a housing development, Negroes have rights equal to those of white persons in obtaining a home or an apartment in that housing development. To illustrate this, a California state court has ruled that qualified Negroes could not be excluded from obtaining homes where financing involved the Federal Housing Administration (FHA) or the Veterans Administration (VA)—both Federal agencies.

One of the first, if not the first, overall national goals in housing was recognized by Congress in the Housing Act of 1949. It stated:

The Congress hereby declares that the general welfare and security of the nation and the health and living standards of its people require housing production and related community development sufficient to remedy the serious housing shortage, the elimination of substandard and other inadequate housing through the clearance of slums and blighted areas, and the realization as soon as feasible of the goal of a decent home and a suitable living environment for every American family, thus contributing to the development and redevelopment of communities and to the advancement of the growth, wealth, and security of the nation.[6]

In the Housing Act, Congress committed the Federal government to a goal of a "decent home" for every American family.

An important development in housing programs occurred in November, 1962, when President Kennedy signed an Executive order barring racial discrimination in any Federally assisted housing program. In more detail, the order bars "discrimination because of race, color, creed, or national origin" as related to the "sale, leasing, rental or other disposition" of any housing that the Federal government owns or operates, that is built with the help of Federal grants or loans, or is financed by Federal mortgage programs, such as FHA.

United States Official Photo

Former President John F. Kennedy speaks to Housing Administrator Robert C. Weaver just prior to signing the Housing Act of 1961. President Lyndon B. Johnson as Vice-President is an interested spectator.

A newer development has private capital building interracial housing units. Experience in this field indicates that both Negro and white persons do buy into such housing units and that they can and do live as good neighbors. Housing units of this nature are developed most frequently in the Middle Atlantic states and the West Coast areas.

It is significant that the number of Negroes who own homes is increasing. In 1940, only 24 percent of nonwhite families were homeowners. By 1960, that figure had risen to 38 percent. This improving condition reflects the Negro's pride in citizenship responsibility, as well as his constantly rising income.

TRANSPORTATION

Obtaining transportation on an equal basis with all other people has always been a problem for the American Negro. The 1896 decision in the case of *Plessy v. Ferguson* was a setback, but in recent years there has been much progress. Where the problem of segregation in the use of transportation facilities persists, it usually involves such restrictions as requiring Negroes to sit in seats at the rear of a bus, or prohibiting Negroes from using bus terminal facilities—waiting rooms, rest rooms, and restaurant areas—designated for white persons. When interstate travel is involved, however, segregation practices no longer are of any major significance. Airlines, in general, have never practiced segregation.

In 1961, the Interstate Commerce Commission took new steps to meet the problem of racial segregation involving interstate bus travel. The Commission prohibited segregation on interstate buses; it prohibited interstate buses from using terminals where segregation was practiced; it stated that buses and terminals must feature signs announcing that their use "is without regard to race, color, or creed." Penalties in the form of fines are provided for violations of these regulations.

PUBLIC ACCOMMODATIONS

About one-half of all the states already had laws forbidding discrimination in the use of public facilities and public accommodations when the Civil Rights Act of 1964 became law. Within six months after passage of the Civil Rights Act, most owners and operators of public facilities and accommodations had moved to comply with the law. There is, however, some resistance in specific areas, particularly in the South. While the

Supreme Court has already handed down several decisions supporting the ban on segregation, it is likely that full compliance with the law is months, perhaps years, away.

PROGRESS IN OBTAINING CIVIL RIGHTS

The problem of civil rights will continue to receive major attention in all areas of the United States. Attorney General Robert Kennedy, speaking in January, 1963, before the tenth anniversary convocation of the Center for the Study of Democratic Institutions, noted that virtually all bus terminals, rail terminals, and airports had been desegregated; that in the preceeding year, officials in twenty-nine counties of four Southern states had voluntarily made voting records available; that there had been eighty-two voting record inspections undertaken by the Justice Department where voluntary action had not been obtained; and that twenty-eight more Southern school districts had been voluntarily desegregated without disturbance.

It must be noted, however, that the record for increased civil rights in the fields of housing, transportation, and public accommodations is not untarnished. One has had only to pick up the daily newspapers in the last few years to read of the "freedom riders" and "sit-ins." These demonstrations, while generally carried on in the spirit of "passive resistance" by the Negroes, have at times erupted into dangerous riots. The struggle for rights in this vital area is continuing.

The Negro
In National Defense

NEGROES AND THE ARMED FORCES

History tells us that Negroes fought for America in all of its wars, from colonial times to the present day. A runaway slave, Crispus Attucks, was one of the first men to die in the Boston Massacre in 1770. Negroes served as soldiers in the Continental Army under George Washington, and also served in the Navy. They fought in the War of 1812, and about 200,000 Negroes were in the Civil War. Abraham Lincoln indicated that Negro troops played an important role in the history of the Union Army. In a letter to General Grant, Lincoln wrote, "I want to take a look at those boys [the Negro troops]. I read . . . of how gallantly [they] behaved . . . they have proved their efficiency."[1]

Two privates, Henry Johnson and Needham Roberts became the first Negro heroes of World War I. Both were awarded the Croix de Guerre by the French government for their actions in turning back a German raid. World War II brought thousands of Negroes into various branches of our armed forces. They fought in all major theatres of the war, beginning with Pearl Harbor to the surrender of Germany and Japan. Negroes also fought in Korea and Viet Nam. Some of America's highest awards—the Congressional Medal of Honor,

Crispus Attucks was fatally wounded in the Boston Massacre in 1770. A monument in his honor has been erected on the Boston Commons.

the Distinguished Service Cross, the Silver Star, and the Distinguished Flying Cross—have been awarded to Negro heroes fighting in the service of their country.

THE AMERICAN REVOLUTION

During the colonial period in America's history, many Negroes openly objected to British troops being placed in the homes of American colonists. The "minutemen" and the colonial forces at the famous Battle of Bunker

The Battle of Quasimas took place near Santiago, Cuba, in June, 1898. The Ninth and Tenth Colored Cavalry is shown in support of the Rough Riders.

Hill included Negroes. During the Battle of Monmouth, June 28, 1778, Negroes fought side by side with white soldiers. Prince Whipple and Oliver Cromwell crossed the Delaware River with George Washington. Some of the other Negro heroes of the American Revolution were Austin Dabney, Lemuel Haynes, and Pompey Lamb.

Not all Negroes fought for the American colonists. Many accepted English offers of freedom from slavery if they would join the British troops. Americans soon recognized the appeal of this approach and tried to counteract it. Washington, for example, enlisted a battalion of Negroes from Rhode Island to bolster his ranks. Rhode Island offered freedom to these slaves for their military services. In many cases, slaves escaped from their masters and joined colonial troops.

THE CIVIL WAR

Civil War heroes included twenty-one Negroes who were awarded the Congressional Medal of Honor. William Carney's participation in the charge against Fort Wagner won him a Medal of Honor. Carney was a member of the Fifty-fourth Massachusetts Volunteers, an all-Negro regiment composed of freemen from the North. Peter Vogelsang of this regiment became one of the first Negroes to rise from an enlisted private to the rank of a commissioned officer. In all, Negroes obtained about seventy-five commissions in the Union Army during the Civil War. During the war, Negroes participated in more than 250 engagements. They were members of the infantry, the heavy artillery, the cavalry, and the navy. By the close of the war, nearly 150 Negro regiments had become a part of our nation's history, and 40,000 Negroes had died.

THE FIRST AND SECOND WORLD WARS

On June 28, 1914, Archduke Francis Ferdinand, heir to the Austrian throne, and his wife were assasinated by Gavrilo Princip at Sarajevo in Bosnia. Within a week, the world-wide conflict we know as World War I began. The United States did not enter the war until April, 1917, but between that time and the end of the war in November, 1918, some 4,700,000 Americans were mobilized for military service. Of this number, about 350,000 were Negroes, and 200,000 of them were sent overseas.

World War II—Pearl Harbor, Bataan, Africa, the Battle of the Bulge, the Coral Sea, D-Day, Iwo Jima, the atom bomb, V-E Day, V-J Day—saw some 700,000 American Negroes in the armed forces with more than 400,000 serving in foreign lands.

Entries in the *United States Congressional Record* in 1944 commented on the part played by the American Negro:

Among the units now fighting in Italy is the Negro Ninety-ninth Pursuit Squadron, which has made an enviable record in dive bombing enemy targets. Three other Negro squadrons, recently arrived on the Italian front, are beginning to demonstrate their effectiveness. One of the most courageous feats now being performed on any battle front is the running of supplies into the Anzio beachhead by quartermaster and trucking units, about 70 percent of them being Negroes, according to Ernie Pyle . . .[2]

The American Negro can be proud of the figure just given out by the War Department as to his part in this war. He has contributed 701,678 men to the army, of whom 411,368 are overseas. There are 5,804 commissioned Negro officers, including dentists, nurses, and other Medical Corps officers and chaplains. It is clear that the Negro has made progress since the last war, both in the types of service open to him and in his educational fitness for them.[3]

THE KOREAN WAR

World War II was followed by the Korean War. Here too, the American Negro produced heroes. For men like

Private First Class William Thompson and Sergeant Cornelius Charlton, posthumously awarded the Congressional Medal of Honor; Second Lieutenant William Benefield, posthumously awarded the Distinguished Service Cross; Colonel Daniel James, awarded the Distinguished Flying Cross; and for many others who served their country equally well, the Korean War was a question of life itself. As in any war, some did not come back. Ensign Jessie Brown was one of these men. The words of Senator Herbert O'Connor of Maryland, and the account which appeared in the *Washington Times-Herald*, tell an eloquent story:

> Ensign Brown met a heroic death. The circumstances attendant upon it should be recorded for the information of all our people throughout the country, it seems to me, as yet another indication of the part which Negro citizens of the United States are playing in the defense of their country today, and of the ready acceptance of their services by their compatriots, regardless of race or color.
>
> I ask unanimous consent that the story from the *Times-Herald* [Washington, December 17, 1950] be reprinted in the Appendix of the [Congressional] *Record*.

There being no objection, the eulogy was ordered to be printed in the *Record*, as follows:

THE UNTOLD STORY
(By Roscoe Simmons)

The death of Ensign Jessie L. Brown of Hattiesburg, Mississippi, who died fighting in the air over Korea for his country, adds another name to the long and distinguished list of colored Mississippians who, for first one thing, then another, achieved a place in the history of American freedom.

Also, Brown's is another picture on the walls of men of color, who, in life or death, proved worthy of the opportunities of their country and the friendship of their white countrymen.

In his heroic death Brown had the tender attention of a white fellow officer, Lt. [j.g.] Thomas J. Hudner, of Massachusetts. Flying a navy fighter, Brown was hit over the Chosan area. Brown made an emergency landing known only to the elements. Hudner, flying and fighting on the same mission, saw Brown touch ground, and began circling the field as protection against enemy attack.

Brown waved his arm as a sign of life but made no attempt to escape from his plane, although it had started burning. Hudner knew that Brown could not free himself and, chancing his own life, landed in the same field. He leaped from his plane and ran to the aid of Brown, but it was too late. Brown was dead.

Lieutenant Hudner radioed for a plane to come for Brown's body and stood by until its arrival and the lifeless form of a comrade was aloft and bound for a camp of friends and fellow warriors.

This is but the continuation of the story, which will never be completely told of the unbroken and fateful relations existing between two people.

The United States Navy feels that the bravery and loyalty of Ensign Brown adds to its long cherished glory. Not only was Brown the only colored naval aviator to fight in Korea, but also the first colored officer of the Navy to lose his life in any war fought by the Union.

The *Congressional Record* statement on the eulogy of Ensign Brown concludes, "Look the world over but our colored people will find their greatest heroism under the Stars and Stripes."[4]

EQUAL OPPORTUNITY IN THE ARMED FORCES

It should be noted that the United States Government has made and is continuing to make a major effort to provide equal opportunities for all persons in the armed forces. A notable example of this was an Executive order issued by President Truman in 1948. This order established a legal basis for a policy of equal treatment and opportunity for all persons in the armed services without regard for race, color, religion, or national origin. President Truman's order stated:

Whereas it is essential that there be maintained in the armed services of the United States the highest standards of democracy, with equality of treatment and opportunity for all those who serve in our country's defense:

Now, therefore, by virtue of the authority vested in me as President of the United States, by the Constitution and the statutes of the United States and as Commander in Chief of the armed services, it is hereby ordered as follows:

1. It is hereby declared to be the policy of the President that there shall be equality of treatment and opportunity for all persons in the armed services without regard to race, color, religion or national origin. This policy shall be put into effect as rapidly as possible, having due regard to the time required to effectuate any necessary changes without impairing efficiency or morale.

2. There shall be created in the National Military Establishment an advisory committee to be known as the President's Committee on Equality of Treatment and Opportunity in the Armed Services, which shall be com-

posed of seven members to be designated by the President.

3. The Committee is authorized on behalf of the President to examine into the rules, procedures and practices of the armed services in order to determine in what respect such rules, procedures and practices may be altered or improved with a view to carrying out the policy of this order. The Committee shall confer and advise with the Secretary of Defense, the Secretary of the Army, the Secretary of the Navy, and the Secretary of the Air Force, and shall make such recommendations to the President and to said Secretaries as in the judgment of the Committee will effectuate the policy hereof.

4. All executive departments and agencies of the Federal Government are authorized and directed to cooperate with the Committee in its work, and to furnish the Committee such information or the services of such persons as the Committee may require in the performance of its duties.

5. When requested by the Committee to do so, persons in the armed services or in any of the executive departments and agencies of the Federal Government shall testify before the Committee and shall make available for the use of the Committee such documents and other information as the Committee may require.

6. The Committee shall continue to exist until such time as the President shall terminate its existence by Executive Order.[5]

Harry S. Truman

The White House, July 26, 1948

As a result of President Truman's order and the efforts of President Eisenhower, by 1958 there were no all-Negro units for servicemen. This was a major step forward when you consider that there had been about 220 such units.

In addition to ending segregation in the armed forces, Executive orders have made it possible for more Negroes to attain higher ranks in the armed forces. Benjamin O. Davis, Jr., holds the distinction of being the highest-ranking Negro officer. In 1959, the Senate confirmed his appointment to the rank of Major General in the United States Air Force. By 1960, there were more than one hundred Negroes holding the rank of Colonel or Lieutenant Colonel in the Army and Air Force. In the regular Navy and among the reserves, there were about two hundred Negro officers with ranks as high as Commander and Lieutenant Commander.

One of the first Negroes to be assigned to a combat ship was Lieutenant Commander Samuel L. Gravely, a graduate of Columbia University's Midshipman's School. Lieutenant Commander Gravely served as commanding officer of the U.S.S. *Falgout,* a destroyer escort ship.

One of the many different national defense structures within which the Negro now serves is SAC—the Strategic Air Command. SAC offers opportunities for both men and women. The Strategic Air Command is the United States Air Force's global striking force. For more than fifteen years it has been one of the world's most powerful military forces operating on a global basis. It deals with global communications and supports systems needed to operate intercontinental weapons, which includes both manned bombers and ballistic missiles. SAC has locations at more than sixty bases in the United States as well as twenty overseas bases. At SAC's March Air Force Base near Riverside, California, two Negroes, Captain Richard L. Biffle, Jr., aircraft commander, and Lieutenant Colonel Leon Creed, navigator, are in continuous readiness to defend our

Lieutenant Commander Samuel L. Gravely as commanding officer of the U. S. S. *Falgout,* a destroyer escort ship.

Official U. S. Navy Photograph

Lieutenant Colonel Leon V. Creed is responsible for periodically checking all navigators of the Strategic Air Command's 22nd Bombardment Wing.

U. S. Air Force Photo

U. S. Air Force Photo

Captain Richard L. Biffle, aircraft commander, with members of his B-47 bomber crew. Left to right: Captain Gordon B. Smith (navigator-bombardier), Captain Biffle, and First Lieutenant Raymond L. Miller (pilot).

93

country. Strategic Air Command forces are on the alert day and night, both in the United States and overseas.

NEGROES AND THE SPACE PROGRAM

Today American Negroes are serving in all phases of the nation's defense programs, not only as members of the armed forces but also as scientists, instructors, technicians, and students. In these capacities, they work in all phases of national defense programs including space research, atomic energy, rockets, missiles, and medicine.

The launching in 1957 of the first man-made satellite marked the beginning of the Space Age. Since that date, the United States has carried on many research projects designed to bring man closer to an understanding of outer space.

Important space research is being directed by the National Aeronautics and Space Administration (NASA). Scientists working in the fields of space medicine, chemistry, physics, physiology, and mathematics, to name a few, have been devoting their efforts toward the launching and maintenance of man in outer space. NASA receives educational and economic support from all military agencies of the Department of Defense, civilian government agencies, and from industry. Since May, 1961, when America's first manned spaceship was launched, NASA has supervised other launchings into space. How is this done? Who are some of the people who are working behind the scenes? In the next few paragraphs, you will read about some of the contributions made by Negroes in this important field.

Colonel Vance Marchbanks performed medical tasks for the original astronauts. The study of the effect of

NASA

As one of the space doctors for the National Aeronautics and Space Administration, Colonel Vance Marchbanks, Jr., was charged with maintaining a constant check on the health of the original astronauts.

conditions in space on the human body is of vital importance in space research. One of the responsibilities of Colonel Marchbanks was to be constantly aware of the health of the astronauts while on land or when orbiting the earth. When the astronauts are in space, a constant check on their health is maintained by the use of complicated electronic devices which are attached to their bodies. These electronic devices relay signals to each monitoring station located around the globe.

Colonel Marchbanks was on duty in Kano, Nigeria, during Colonel Glenn's flight in February, 1962. Less than one-half hour after Glenn's launching, the astronaut passed over the Kano monitoring station. During the few minutes that Glenn was over this area, his physical condition was analyzed by Colonel Marchbanks. After the data were studied, a report was sent to Cape Canaveral (now Cape Kennedy)—the headquarters for Project Mercury. Each time Glenn passed over Kano, Marchbanks and his fellow researchers were required to make important decisions about the operations of the space flight.

Colonel Marchbanks, chief flight surgeon, has been in the Air Force for more than fifteen years. He has more than fifteen hundred flying hours to his credit, and earned the Bronze Star as group surgeon with the 332nd Flight Group stationed in Italy during World War II. In 1960, Marchbanks was assigned to Project Mercury because of his outstanding work in aviation medical research. One of his studies showed that the adrenal hormone content in human tissue and blood can serve as an indicator of physical fatigue. This was important, because it was often found to be a factor in the condition of pilots preceding a crash. This research earned Colonel Marchbanks the Air Force Commendation Medal. His work in Project Mercury has helped America acquire newer information about the reaction of the human body under space travel conditions.

Captain Edward Joseph Dwight, Jr., is the first Negro in the astronaut training program. Captain Dwight dreamed of being a pilot when he was a young boy in Kansas City. There he was the first Negro boy to attend Ward Catholic High School, where he was a star halfback on the football team, a member of the track team, and was elected to the National Honor Society. He studied engineering at Kansas City Junior College and then joined the Air Force. Dwight earned his Air

Captain Edward J. Dwight, Jr., the first Negro astronaut trainee, is currently one of a number of pilots working in the Air Force's X-20 Dyna-Soar program at the Air Force Flight Test Center, Edwards Air Force Base, California.

Force Wings in 1955 and continued his education at Arizona State University, where he was awarded, "with distinction," a degree in aeronautical engineering.

Melba L. Roy programs scientific problems for NASA. Before a space vehicle is launched, its anticipated trip or flight path must be accurately plotted. The flight plan must provide for keeping the vehicle in its correct orbital path. The position of the vehicle can be determined by "tracking" it with radio and optical equipment on earth. One of the important research centers for NASA is Goddard Space Flight Center in Washington, D. C. It is in this center that Mrs. Roy, a mathematician,

NASA

Mrs. Melba Roy, Jessie L. Morrey, and Patrick Gorman review orbital calculations from the 7090 computer system at Goddard Space Flight Center.

works as section head of the Program Production Section of the Advanced Orbital Programming Branch. One of her first assignments was with the Tracking and Data Systems of NASA.

Emmett W. Chappelle suggested a solution to the problem of carbon monoxide in space ships. Chappelle, a biochemist, believes that "unlocking the secrets of green plants may be a key to man's survival in prolonged space travel." In searching for these secrets, Chappelle, a

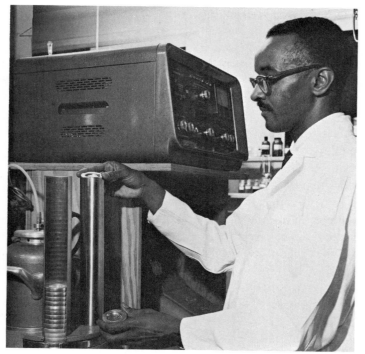

RIAS, Martin Company, Baltimore, Md.

Emmett Chappelle is a research chemist at the Research Institute for Advanced Study (Martin Company, Baltimore, Md.). His research is directed toward the protection of space explorers.

research scientist at the Martin Company's Research Institute for Advanced Study (RIAS), in Baltimore, has uncovered a possible solution to the problem of protecting space explorers from deadly carbon monoxide produced within the ship by electrical systems, fuel combustion units, and the space travelers themselves.

In his research, supported by the Air Force School of Aviation Medicine at Brooks Air Force Base, Texas, Chappelle found that Chlorella, a rather common green algae, has the ability to convert the deadly gas, carbon monoxide, into its harmless relative, carbon dioxide. Among the higher plants, the most effective agent for rendering carbon monoxide harmless is the cucumber.

Prior to joining the RIAS staff in 1958, Chappelle taught biochemistry at Meharry Medical College, Nashville, Tennessee, and served as a research associate while engaged in graduate study at Stanford University.

Chappelle, in his basic research with the photosyntheses group at RIAS, is not seeking the most efficient plants nor is he attempting to develop a conversion system. Rather, he is striving to arrive at a better understanding of the mechanism whereby green plants perform this conversion. This answer would add still another dimension to man's understanding of his environment in the Space Age.

The scientific contributions to space research by Colonel Marchbanks, Captain Dwight, Melba Roy, and Emmett Chappelle, are examples of ways in which the Negro is helping in the defense of the United States. In addition to the activities already mentioned, Negroes are engaged in many other kinds of space work, such as research in airborne armament control systems designed to intercept enemy planes and in space antennas designed for soft-lunar landing vehicles.

Current Negro Protests

The fires of frustration and discord are burning in every city, North and South. Where legal remedies are not at hand, redress is sought in the streets in demonstrations, parades and protests, which create tensions and threaten violence—and threaten lives.

We face, therefore, a moral crisis as a country and as a people. It cannot be met by repressive police action. It cannot be left to increased demonstrations in the streets. It cannot be quieted by token moves or talk. It is time to act in the Congress, in your state and local legislative body, and above all, in all of our daily lives.[1]

—PRESIDENT JOHN F. KENNEDY

Negro leaders started a new type of movement during the 1950s, when they decided to demonstrate openly for full citizenship rights "here and now." While continuing to achieve goals through court action, the American Negro gave added emphasis to non-violent, direct action. As a result, such terms as demonstrations, marches, boycotts, sit-ins, freedom rides, and civil rights legislation, have assumed major importance in the lives of all of us.

On August 28, 1963, some 200,000 persons—Negro and Caucasian—marched in Washington, D.C. They carried signs with slogans reading, "We Want Our Freedom—And We Want It Now!"

Why this march on Washington? The march was a climax of Negro protest against a century-old denial of first-class citizenship rights guaranteed by the Constitution. To understand the full meaning of the march on Washington, one needs to recall some of the significant protest movements that occurred before this climactic nationwide protest.

THE NATURE OF PROTEST MOVEMENTS

It is a constitutional right of the people to peaceably assemble, and to petition the government for a redress of grievances. During the late 1950s and into the 1960s, the American Negro increasingly sought redress of grievances against existing forms of segregation and discrimination in the areas of (1) public school education, (2) employment, (3) housing, (4) public accommodations and recreational facilities, (5) intrastate bus transportation, and (6) voting registration. Protest movements were planned to achieve full citizenship rights in these various areas of living. Action was in the form of demonstrations such as: *sit-ins, pray-ins, jail-ins, freedom rides, boycotts,* and *freedom marches.*

Participants in all types of protests included persons from different ethnic groups, age levels, and occupational groups—college students, professors, school children, housewives, industrial and agricultural workers, clergymen, and celebrities from many areas of the arts and sciences.

PURPOSE OF THE PROTEST MOVEMENTS

Why these protest movements and public demonstrations? Nationwide the technique is used to bring about political, social, economic, and educational

Some 125 Negro and white demonstrators held a prayer vigil in Cambridge, Maryland, on July 8, 1963. The group marched from the Negro section, singing and clapping in the first demonstration after the National Guard troops were ordered into the racially torn town on June 13.

103

change *now*. Leaders of the protest movements have indicated that the demonstrations must continue until the full rights guaranteed by the Federal Constitution are granted to the American Negro. These leaders have noted that protest movements have succeeded in many cases where other approaches have failed.

Let us look at a few examples of more highly publicized events which resulted from several different kinds of protests.

BOYCOTTS

The Montgomery, Alabama, bus boycott (1955-56) was one of the first freedom protest movements engaged in by the Negro.

In Montgomery, Negro bus passengers were required by law to give up their seats to Caucasian passengers. It was, therefore, not unusual for a bus driver to order a Negro passenger to give up his or her seat to a Caucasian passenger who had boarded the bus. It was unusual, however, for a Negro passenger to refuse to obey the order. Mrs. Rosa Parks refused to give up her seat, and because of her refusal, she was arrested and fined ten dollars. This event led to the Montgomery bus boycott and the emergence of one of the leaders in the protest movements, Dr. Martin Luther King, Jr. The boycott, led by Dr. King, received strong community support. During this boycott, Dr. King's home was bombed. In November, 1956, the United States Supreme Court declared that ordinances requiring segregation in intrastate buses are unconstitutional.

SIT-INS

The longest sit-in campaign on record was staged by the Oklahoma City Youth Council of the National Association for the Advancement of Colored People under the guidance of Mrs. Clara Luper. This sit-in campaign began in 1958, and after five years the demonstrations brought about the desegregation of over 120 stores, hotels, lunch counters, and motels. In addition, progress was made in securing equal job opportunities for Negroes.

In March, 1960, Nashville, Tennessee, was the scene of sit-in demonstrations at several eating places by students from Fisk University. The students were arrested and charged with conspiracy to obstruct trade. By May, 1960, however, the lunch counters in downtown Nashville were integrated. At the same time an economic boycott was being carried on by the adults of Nashville. After several months, the merchants and boycotters agreed to negotiate their differences. Other sit-ins at Nashville developed in later years.

In 1963, at Charleston, South Carolina, a two-month protest movement saw the arrest of more than eight hundred persons for picketing and staging sit-ins in various business establishments. The result of the campaign was an agreement with ninety merchants to cooperate in a six-point program which included equal job opportunities and desegregation of public facilities.

FREEDOM RIDES

In September, 1961, the Interstate Commerce Commission issued an order banning segregation in the facilities of interstate transportation terminals. This order followed a series of freedom rides, which began in May, 1961. The first freedom ride originated at Washington, D.C. and ended in Jackson, Mississippi, where its sponsor, James Farmer, director of the Congress of Racial Equality (CORE), was arrested. Upon conclusion of the ride, another was started, this time sponsored by Dr. King's group, the Southern Christian Leadership Conference. The freedom riders were college students who rode from Nashville to Birmingham. In front of the Birmingham bus terminal, the freedom riders were attacked and beaten. Ten freedom riders and five sympathizers were arrested and placed in jail. About this same time, another group of freedom riders boarded a bus enroute to Montgomery, Alabama. Upon arrival there, violence erupted. It was necessary for the United States Attorney General to order Federal marshals into Montgomery to restore order. As a result of the freedom rides, the Interstate Commerce Commission issued an order banning segregation in interstate terminal facilities.

DEMONSTRATIONS

Accounts of the Birmingham demonstration which began in April, 1963, appeared in newspapers and magazines in most sections of the world. It was led by Dr. King. Men, women and children paraded into the downtown section of the city to protest against (1) segregated restaurants and drinking fountains; (2) discriminatory employment practices; and (3) segregated public schools, public parks, and other public facilities. Demonstrators were arrested at lunch counters, on downtown streets or wherever they gathered in groups within the city. It was on Sunday, May 7, 1963, that the protest movement faced a crisis. On this day, several hundred persons left a church and walked through a police line which had been set up near the church to prevent them from marching into downtown Birmingham. The Commissioner of Public Safety ordered fire hoses turned on the marchers. The force of the water pressure swept men, women, and children down the street. More than three thousand persons, including Dr. King, were jailed, during these Birmingham demonstrations.

While Dr. King was in jail, a group of Caucasian clergymen wrote a public statement criticizing him, in

106

effect, for "unwise and untimely" demonstrations. His reply to this criticism is best known as the "Letter from Birmingham Jail." Dr. King's letter, written on bits of paper obtained from whatever source was available to him in jail, received nationwide attention. It was acclaimed a classic example of literature expressing the nature of the 1963 Negro revolution. The following excerpts are taken from his letter:

Injustice anywhere is a threat to justice everywhere . . .

You may well ask, "Why direct action? Why sit-ins, marches, and so forth? Isn't negotiation a better path?" You are quite right in calling for negotiation. Indeed, this is the very purpose of direct action. Non-violent direct action seeks to create such a crisis and foster such a tension that a community which has constantly refused to negotiate is forced to confront the issue. It seeks so to dramatize the issue that it can no longer be ignored . . .

We know through painful experience that freedom is never voluntarily given by the oppressor . . . For years now I have heard the word "Wait!" It rings in the ears of every Negro . . . This "wait" has almost always meant "Never" . . . We have waited for more than 340 years for our constitutional and God-given rights . . .

Perhaps it is easy for those who have never felt the stinging darts of segregation to say "Wait." But when . . . you suddenly find your tongue twisted and your speech stammering as you seek to explain to your six-year-old daughter why she can't go to the public amusement park that has just been advertised on television, and see tears welling up in her eyes when she is told that Funtown is closed to colored children, and see ominous clouds of inferiority begin to form in her little mental sky, and see her beginning to distort her personality by developing an unconscious bitterness toward white peo- ple . . . when you take a cross-country drive and find it necessary to sleep night after night in the uncom- fortable corners of your automobile because no motel will accept you; when you are humiliated day in and day out by nagging signs reading "white" and "colored," . . . then you will understand why we find it difficult to wait . . .

Of course there is nothing new about this kind of civil disobedience . . . It was practiced superbly by the early Christians, who were willing to face hungry lions and the excrutiating pain of chopping blocks rather than submit to certain unjust laws of the Roman Empire . . .

We must use time creatively, in the knowledge that the time is always ripe to do right. Now is the time to make real the promise of democracy and transform our pend- ing national elegy into a creative psalm of brotherhood. Now is the time to lift our national policy from the quicksand of racial injustice to the solid rock of human dignity . . .

Oppressed people cannot remain oppressed forever. The yearning for freedom eventually manifests itself, and that is what has happened to the American Negro . . .

. . . Let us all hope that the dark clouds of racial prejudice will soon pass away and the deep fog of mis- understanding will be lifted from our fear-drenched com- munities, and in some not too distant tomorrow the radiant stars of love and brotherhood will shine over our great nation with all their scintillating beauty.

"Letter from Birmingham Jail" (*April 16, 1963*) *from* WHY WE CAN'T WAIT *by Martin Luther King, Jr. Copy- right © 1963 by Martin Luther King, Jr. Reprinted with the permission of Harper & Row, Publishers, Incorporated.*

Although the leaders of the freedom movement at Birmingham were pledged to nonviolent, direct action, there were persons who responded to nonviolence with violence. A freedom walker was killed. A church was bombed killing four children, and on the same day two teenagers were shot while riding their bicycles.

DE FACTO SEGREGATION

Demonstrations, boycotts, and sit-ins were also used to protest against *de facto* segregation in public schools. California, Ohio, Indiana, Massachusetts, New York, and other states in the North and West were confronted with problems concerned with *de facto* segregation. The term *de facto* means that something exists in fact and in opposition to that which is assumed to exist. It is the position of the Negro that although school people may assume that desegregation is in effect, actually segregation is the real state of affairs.

In many Northern and Western cities there are schools that have all or nearly all Negro enrollments. When these schools are operated within a school district which has a policy of desegregation, *de facto* segregation may be said to exist. On the one hand, school people may say that the all-colored enrollments in these schools are due only to the fact that the neighborhood school is in a Negro community. On the other hand, the Negro may say that this school district is in fact, operating segregated schools.

Some examples of action taken by school boards to eliminate *de facto* segregation include: (1) an "open enrollment" policy, which provides that a school with unused space will accept some students from other areas, with the parents usually accepting responsibility for student transportation; (2) a periodic review of neighborhood school boundaries and readjustment when necessary; and (3) free bus transportation for students who are attending schools in an area other than their own neighborhood. At present these practices are not used widely. They simply indicate attempts by some school districts to deal effectively with the problem of *de facto* segregation.

Court decisions in cases involving *de facto* segregation have varied widely. The California Supreme Court took the position that ". . . the right to an equal opportunity for education and the harmful consequences of segregation require that school boards take steps to alleviate racial imbalance in schools regardless of its cause." In contrast, a Federal court in Indiana took the position that school boards have no affirmative duty to end racial imbalance in school systems when that imbalance results from community patterns rather than by law or design. The Indiana case was appealed to the Supreme Court, which refused to review the decision.

FREEDOM MARCH

The march on Washington, previously mentioned, was generally a nonviolent, peaceful, and dignified protest. The march was planned as one way of demonstrating to the nation's leaders the urgent need for meaningful Civil Rights legislation. It was a demonstration that included the cooperation of many agencies. Volunteer workers from the National Council of Churches made up 80,000 box lunches and sold them for only fifty cents to the marchers. The District of Columbia police offered the protection of motorcycle escorts, and the United States Army offered the use of 4,000 troops in case an emergency situation developed. The Washington Senators baseball team postponed two of its scheduled games. It was estimated that some 200,000 persons heard Dr. King, Roy L. Wilkins, A. Phillip Randolph, and others call for freedom, justice, and equality for the Negro NOW. Wilkins, executive secretary of the National Association for the Advancement of Colored People, on sensing the human dignity of the marchers was moved to say, "I am so proud of my people."

THE CIVIL RIGHTS ACT OF 1964

In June, 1963, in the midst of the protest movement, President Kennedy asked Congress to enact legislation enforcing for all citizens such rights as the right to vote, the right to be served in public facilities, and the right to equal public education and job opportunities. After months of debate, the Civil Rights Act was finally passed by Congress and signed by President Johnson on July 2, 1964. (See the Appendix for a summary of the act.)

FREEDOM MOVEMENT ORGANIZATIONS

From the above discussion of freedom movements, it is apparent that progress has been made. Among the best-known organized groups that use the technique of nonviolent demonstrations are: the National Association for the Advancement of Colored People (NAACP), The National Urban League, the Southern Christian Leadership Conference (SCLC), the Student Nonviolent Coordinating Committee ("SNICK"), and the Congress of Racial Equality (CORE).

NATIONAL ASSOCIATION FOR
THE ADVANCEMENT OF COLORED PEOPLE

Thirteen years after the Supreme Court made its ruling in *Plessy v. Ferguson,* the National Association for the Advancement of Colored People was founded.

Martin Luther King, Jr., a Baptist minister, is a native of Atlanta, Georgia. He was graduated from Morehouse College, Crozer Theological Seminary, Boston University, and the Chicago Theological Seminary. In 1954, he became pastor of the Dexter Avenue Baptist Church in Montgomery, Alabama.

Johnson Publishing Company

Johnson Publishing Company

Whitney M. Young, Jr., executive director of the National Urban League since 1961, was born in Lincoln Ridge, Kentucky. A graduate of Kentucky State College and the University of Minnesota, Young was Dean of the School of Social Work at Atlanta University from 1954 to 1960.

112

Roy Wilkins was born in St. Louis and is a graduate of the University of Minnesota. He was editor of *The Crisis,* the official publication of the NAACP, from 1934 to 1949. Wilkins became executive secretary of the NAACP in 1955.

Johnson Publishing Company

James Farmer is a native of Marshall, Texas. He graduated from Wiley College at the age of eighteen. He received a Bachelor of Divinity degree from Howard University, but refused to be ordained as a Methodist minister because of segregation in Methodist churches in the South.

The *Plessy* case, discussed in a previous section, involved the separate but equal doctrine that many states used to enforce segregation, not only in matters of transportation but also in social, political, religious, economic, and educational affairs. The NAACP played a major role in obtaining the United States Supreme Court school desegregation decision of 1954 which reversed the *Plessy v. Ferguson* decision.

The NAACP is the oldest and largest of all organized groups devoted to attaining full citizenship rights for the American Negro. The general objectives of the NAACP include:

1. anti-lynching legislation;
2. legislation to end peonage and debt slavery among the sharecroppers and tenant farmers of the South;
3. enfranchisement of the Negro in the South;
4. abolition of injustices in legal procedure, particularly criminal procedure, based solely upon color or race;
5. equitable distribution of funds for public education;
6. abolition of segregation, discrimination, insult, and humiliation based on race or color;
7. equality of opportunity to work in all fields with equal pay for equal work;
8. abolition of discrimination against Negroes in the right to collective bargaining through membership in labor unions.

Since its beginning in 1909, the NAACP has emphasized the use of the courts in its drive to obtain full citizenship rights for the American Negro. In recent years, the NAACP has taken an active part in direct-action movements, as well as continuing its efforts to obtain legal action on civil rights. For example, in 1963 at Philadelphia, the organization picketed a school construction job. The picket line was protesting alleged bias against Negroes in labor unions. Following a four-day demonstration, the unions agreed to accept some Negroes in skilled construction jobs. Roy L. Wilkins is the executive secretary of the NAACP with headquarters in New York City.

NATIONAL URBAN LEAGUE

For many years the purpose of the National Urban League was to train the Negro for employment opportunities, and to acquaint prospective employers with his ability for other than menial occupations. The organization was successful in finding employment for many persons. However, discriminatory hiring practices frequently defeated the league's efforts. In the 1960s, the organization joined other freedom groups in the fight for full citizenship rights as well as continuing with its employment aims. Whitney M. Young, Jr., director of the league, has outlined the current program to include reducing the rate of unemployment among Negroes, obtaining better housing conditions, and training the Negro in skills required to meet the demands of an automated economy.

SOUTHERN CHRISTIAN LEADERSHIP CONFERENCE

This organization is dedicated to helping the American Negro attain first-class citizenship by nonviolent action and education. Dr. Martin Luther King, Jr., its founder and leader, was named by *Time* magazine as the Man of the Year in 1963, and in 1964 was awarded the Nobel Peace Prize. Dr. King, at thirty-five years of age, was the youngest person ever to receive this coveted award.

Dr. King is regarded by most persons as the symbol of the 1963 Negro revolution in the United States. His use of nonviolent, direct action, based in part upon the

115

philosophy of Mahatma Gandhi, was mentioned in connection with the Montgomery bus boycott.

In 1957, Dr. King organized the Southern Christian Leadership Conference and became its leader. As other freedom groups planned sit-ins and other forms of demonstrations, Dr. King's group helped organize and supported their activities. One of the major purposes of assisting in the organization of these groups was to train volunteers in the techniques of using nonviolent, direct action.

In Birmingham, Alabama, Dr. King was once again in the limelight as he was during the Montgomery bus boycott. It was at Birmingham that Dr. King moved into a major leadership position in the Negro revolution. Here, as a leader, Dr. King sought to assure a successful nonviolent demonstration aimed at improving social, economic, and educational conditions.

The purposes of the Southern Christian Leadership Conference as summarized in its literature are: (1) to obtain increased voter registration (Southwide); (2) to hold citizenship clinics and workshops on nonviolence; (3) to use direct action projects to end segregation; (4) to obtain merit employment programs to end job discrimination; (5) to provide special educational scholarships; (6) to provide legal defense and bail for victims of racial injustice; and (7) to conduct citizenship and literacy schools.

STUDENT NONVIOLENT COORDINATING COMMITTEE

John Henry Lewis, a 1963 graduate of Fisk University in Nashville, Tennessee, was one of the founders of this organization. Lewis served as the national chairman of this college youth inspired group. It was Lewis and some of his fellow students who staged the sit-in demonstrations at the lunch counters in Nashville in 1960.

These demonstrations were based, in part, on the philosophy that the erection of segregated barriers is an affront to the dignity of Negroes. The organization is dedicated to the eradication of all symbols of segregation.

CONGRESS OF RACIAL EQUALITY

This organization was formed in 1942 in New York City and rose to prominence with the freedom riders of 1961. James L. Farmer, one of the founders, became its national chairman. Farmer is considered by some writers as a pioneer in the development and expansion of nonviolent, direct-action techniques of fighting segregation and discriminatory practices. Plans for the organizations current nationwide program include: (1) the elimination of *de facto* segregation in schools; (2) the abolition of segregated housing patterns in the North; (3) the removal of voting restrictions; (4) gaining free access to public accommodations; and (5) obtaining equal job opportunities in the South.

UNITED COUNCIL FOR CIVIL RIGHTS LEADERSHIP

This is the latest freedom movement group, having been organized in July, 1963. The Council includes all the groups discussed in the preceding paragraphs plus the National Council of Negro Women.

GOALS AND PURPOSES

In any discussion of the freedom movement organizations, it should be emphasized that they do not advocate or approve of irresponsibly led demonstrations by any of their individual chapters. They objected, for example, to the plans by the Brooklyn chapter of CORE to stage "car stall-ins" on major highways leading to the New York World's Fair. Because of its refusal to abandon those plans, the Brooklyn chapter was suspended by the national CORE organization.

The ultimate goal of each of these organizations is to continue the fight for full freedom and equality of the American Negro—freedom and equality guaranteed by the United States Constitution. Gains have been made, but leaders of these organizations agree that much remains to be done before it can be said that the American Negro has, in fact, secured the rights granted by the Constitution.

Prospects for the Future

The American Negro's goal of full citizenship rights is coming closer to reality with each passing year. As you have learned from reading the previous chapters, progress has been slow but certain. The steady march of progress can be seen when you study the history of our country, especially the history of recent decades. The many gains that have been made should serve as the basis for future progress.

As Negroes are given more opportunities to make their contributions, more will succeed. As these successes increase and become known, new concepts and ideas about the Negro people will develop.

The history of the American Negro has been an important part of the history of progress and of the history of our country. As social and economic opportunities for the Negro increase, there is every reason to believe that he will make even greater contributions to American culture.

The decade of the 1960s has been called by some observers the "Decade of Revolution." One phase of this movement has been a continuous revolution within the borders of our own country. And this revolution has concerned the very same American Negro that we have been talking about. For the most part, it has been a peaceful revolution. And unlike some revolutions in the past, its goals are those to which every American should fully subscribe. It is the story of the struggle of some 19 million American Negroes for those rights which other Americans have enjoyed for many years.

Summary

The American Negro must be thought of as many different people. All of them do not think alike, do not perform the same kind of work, or live in the same way. They differ among themselves just as any other group. They cannot be stereotyped.

The Negro is making progress in his search for civil rights. During the past 100 years, he has obtained his freedom and his citizenship, and his right to vote has been guaranteed by our Federal Constitution. He has obtained certain rights to work, rights equal to those of other persons. He has witnessed a Supreme Court decision that grants him equal educational opportunities. He has acquired a better home, his income has risen, and his right to use public accommodations has been increased and strengthened. White and colored people are working together, studying together, and in some areas, using the same recreational facilities.

Many forces are and have been at work to improve the status of the American Negro and to accelerate his progress. Some of these forces include our Federal government, the international situation, the economic situation, education, war, and the threat of war. Both major political parties have strengthened their "planks" in statements concerning the Negro. Both parties have supported legislation to improve civil rights. Other countries are watching to see how America and the Negro relate. This is one of the factors that has caused many American citizens to evaluate more closely the effects of segregation and to support the move toward full citizenship rights.

We are living in prosperous times and the Negro is prospering along with others. Business and labor leaders are working to provide more and better employment opportunities for all qualified persons. In the field of education, integration is occurring on a broader scale each year. More schools are opening their doors to the Negro, and he is realizing the need for becoming better educated. World War II required the use of all of America's manpower. As a result, jobs were opened to more people. Today the threat of a nuclear war makes it imperative that this nation make the best possible use of all its intellectual and physical manpower.

The Negro has shown faith in the American way of life. For the most part, he has trusted his problems and concerns to the justice of America's courts. As a result, the movement toward equal opportunities for all persons has been accelerated. Hopefully, the time is not far off when each person's contribution to the society in which he lives will be limited only by his abilities and his willingness to make the best possible use of his talents.

REFERENCES

THE NEGRO SEEKS CITIZENSHIP

1   *U. S. News and World Report*, June 11, 1962, pp. 56-57.

SEPARATE BUT EQUAL

1   *The Supreme Court Reporter*, West Publishing Company, St. Paul, Minn., 1896, vol. 16, pp. 1138-1148.

SECURING AN EDUCATION

1   Henry Steele Commager, (ed.), *Documents of American History*, Appleton-Century-Crofts, Inc., New York, 1958, 6th Ed., p. 801.
2   "Public School Desegregation," *Southern School News*, May, 1964, vol. 10:11, p. 1.
3   U. S. Department of Labor, *The Economic Situation of Negroes in the United States*, 1962, Bulletin S-3, p. 27.
4   U. S. Department of Commerce, *Statistical Abstract of the United States*, 1964, p. 111.

EARNING A LIVING

1   U. S. Department of Labor, *The Economic Situation of Negroes in the United States*, 1962, Bulletin S-3, p. 9.
2   U. S. Department of Commerce, *Statistical Abstract of the United States*, 1964, p. 30.
3   U. S. Department of Labor, *op. cit.*, p. 7.
4   *Ibid.*
5   U. S. Commission on Civil Rights, *Employment*, 1961, p. 157.
6   Burnell Phillips, "This Week with Riverside County Labor," *The Press-Enterprise*, Riverside, California, Nov. 25, 1962.
7   U. S. Department of Labor *op. cit.*, p. 8.
8   *Federal Register*, "Executive Order 8802," 1941, vol. 6, no. 125.

9   U. S. Department of Labor, *op. cit.*, pp. 15, 17.
10 Jessie Guzman, ed., *Negro Yearbook: A Review of Events Affecting Negro Life, 1941-1946*, Department of Records and Research, Tuskegee Institute, Tuskegee, Alabama, 1947, p. 33.
11 Emma Sterne, *Blood Brothers: Four Men of Science*, Alfred A. Knopf, Inc., New York, 1959.
12 U. S. Department of Commerce, *op. cit.*, p. 30.

HOUSING, TRANSPORTATION, AND PUBLIC ACCOMMODATIONS

1   Luigi Laurenti, *Property Values and Race: Studies in Seven Cities*, University of California, Berkeley and Los Angeles, 1960, pp. 3-4.
2   *Ibid.*, p. 47.
3   *Ibid.*, p. 236.
4   U. S. Commission on Civil Rights, *Housing*, 1961, p. 140.
5   *Ibid.*, p. 145.
6   *Ibid.*, pp. 19-20.

THE NEGRO IN NATIONAL DEFENSE

1   J. A. Rogers, *The Civil War Centennial — 100 Years Later*, p. 3. (Copies available from J. A. Rogers, 37 Morningside Avenue, New York.)
2   *U. S. Congressional Record*, 1944, app., vol. 90, pt. 9, p. A-2927.
3   *Ibid.*, pt. 2, p. A-4734.
4   *Ibid.*, 1950-1951, vol. 96, pt. 18, p. A-7790.
5   *Federal Register,* "Executive Order 9981," 1948, p. 4313.

CURRENT NEGRO PROTESTS

1   John F. Kennedy, "A Moral Imperative — Equality of Treatment," *Vital Speeches of the Day*, July 1, 1963, vol. 29, pp. 546-547.

SUGGESTED READING ON SPECIFIC TOPICS

CIVIL RIGHTS

"Races," *Time*, June 21, 1963, vol. 81:25, pp. 13-17.

"A Legal History of Negro Progress," *Time*, June 21, 1963, vol. 81:25, p. 15.

"The Negro in America," *Newsweek*, July 29, 1963, vol. 62, pp. 15-41.

"Civil Rights," *Time*, Sept. 6, 1963, vol. 82:10, pp. 13-15.

"Civil Rights," *Time*, Sept. 27, 1963, vol. 82:13, pp. 17-21.

"What the Marchers Really Want," *The New York Times Magazine*, Aug. 25, 1963, pp. 7-9, 57-61.

NEGRO REVOLUTION

"Civil Rights," *Time*, Aug. 30, 1963, vol. 82:9, pp. 9-14.

EMANCIPATION PROCLAMATION

Ebony, Sept., 1963, vol. 18:11; a special issue in commemoration of the 100th anniversary of The Emancipation Proclamation.

SCHOOL DESEGREGATION

Southern School News, Oct., 1962; Nov., 1962; Feb., 1963; Aug., 1963; Sept., 1963; Oct., 1963; May, 1964.

"Negro Leaders Tell Their Plans for '64," *U.S. News and World Report*, Feb., 24, 1964, vol. 56, pp. 56-62, 67-71.

A SUMMARY OF THE PROVISIONS OF
THE CIVIL RIGHTS ACT OF 1964

The following is based, in part, on a summary appearing in The National Observer *and is reprinted by permission of that publication.*

TITLE I

Voting Rights. Outlaws racial discrimination in qualification of voters for Federal elections. Prohibits denial of voting rights in Federal elections because of registration errors "not material" in determining voter qualification. Forbids literacy tests as qualifications for voting in Federal elections unless such tests are administered in writing to all voters and a copy of the test a voter has taken, and the answers, are provided the voter requesting them within 25 days after his request. Provides that literacy "shall be a rebuttable presumption" if a would-be voter has completed the sixth grade in school.

Authorizes the U.S. Attorney General or a defendant in a voting case to request a three-judge Federal court to hear cases in which the Attorney General seeks a finding that a pattern or practice of discrimination exists. Under a prior law, which Title I is supplementing, once the court finds a pattern or practice of discrimination, a person affected by the discrimination is entitled to an order declaring him qualified to vote upon proof that 1) he is qualified under state law, and 2) he has, since the finding by the court, been denied under color of law the opportunity to register to vote or has been found not qualified to vote by any person acting under color of law. Prior law also provides for the appointment of voting referees to hear the applications of persons claiming denial of their right to vote and to make a report to the court. Authorizes appeal from a three-judge court directly to the U.S. Supreme Court on the question of whether a pattern or practice of discrimination exists.

TITLE II

Injunctive Relief Against Discrimination in Places of Public Accommodation. Bars discrimination and segregation in places of public accommodation such as inns, hotels, motels, restaurants, lunch counters, theaters, sports arenas, service stations, and concert halls if interstate commerce is affected, or if such discrimination is supported by state action.

According to this title, interstate commerce is affected if "a substantial portion" of goods sold or exhibited move in interstate commerce or if the accommodations in question are on the premises of an establishment involved in interstate commerce (e.g., a restaurant in a train station). Discrimination is supported by state action when it is carried on under color of state or local law, or required by state or local executive or administrative action, or carried on under color of custom or usage enforced by state officials.

Specifically exempted from this provision are private clubs and rooming houses with no more than five rooms for hire, when the proprietor is a resident.

Makes state and local laws permitting or requiring discrimination or segregation in places of public accommodation covered by this title unenforceable by prohibiting attempts to punish persons who attempt to exercise the right of freedom from segregation and discrimination in public accommodations.

Permits an aggrieved person to seek protection of a Federal court order in a civil action "whenever any person has engaged or there are reasonable grounds to believe that any person is about to engage" in acts prohibited under this title. Authorizes the court to permit the Attorney General to intervene in a civil action by an individual if he certifies that the case is of general public importance.

Prohibits any civil action seeking such court orders . . . for 30 days from the time of complaint in states or communities where the alleged discriminatory practices are prohibited by local law.

Permits the court, in states where alleged discriminatory practices are not covered by local or state law, to defer civil . . . action for as long as 120 days while the matter is referred to the Community Relations Service established by Title X of this bill, if the court believes there is a possibility of obtaining voluntary compliance with provisions of this title.

Requires the Community Relations Service to conduct closed hearings when such complaints are referred to it and no testimony shall be released except by agreement of all parties involved in the complaint with the permission of the court.

In addition to intervening in a civil action by an individual, the Attorney General is authorized to bring a civil action seeking a permanent or temporary injunction when he has reasonable cause to believe that any person or group of persons is engaged in a pattern or practice of resistance to the enjoyment of the rights secured by the title. Permits the Attorney General to ask for a three-judge Federal court to hear cases covered by this section.

This request must be accompanied by a certificate saying the case "is of general public importance." Authorizes appeal from a three-judge court under this section directly to the U.S. Supreme Court.

Desegregation of Public Facilities. Authorizes the Attorney General to file civil suits to end discrimination or segregation in public facilities, except schools, owned, operated or managed by state or local governments, upon receipt of complaints by aggrieved persons, if he believes the complaints have merit and the persons making the complaints are unable to bear the costs of filing the suits or would be physically endangered or financially hurt by filing such suits.

Desegregation of Public Education. Orders the U.S. commissioner of education to conduct a survey of "the lack of availability of equal educational opportunities for individuals by reason of race, color, religion, or national origin" in public schools, and report his finding to Congress and the President within two years from enactment of the title.

Authorizes the commissioner to provide technical assistance, such as advice on special educational problems, to states, school boards, and schools in order to implement desegregation. Authorizes the commissioner to make Federal funds available to facilitate training of teachers and administrators to cope with problems of desegregation.

Authorizes the Attorney General, upon receipt of a complaint that an individual has been refused admission or has not been permitted to continue in attendance at a public college by reason of race, color, religion, or national origin, or a complaint that a school board has deprived children of equal protection of the laws, to file suit on behalf of that person, under certain conditions, if he believes that the legal action will materially further the orderly achievement of desegregation in public education. The Attorney General must certify that the complainant is unable to initiate and maintain the action, a judgment that may be based on the inability of a person to bear the costs of the suit, or the jeopardizing, in the Attorney General's opinion, of the personal safety or economic standing of the person by his filing such suit. Notice must first be given to the school board or appropriate college authority to give them reasonable time to adjust such complaints.

This title specifically declares that "desegregation shall not mean the assignment of students to public schools in order to overcome racial imbalance," and it is further stated in the section authorizing suits by the Attorney General, "nothing herein shall empower any official or court of the United States to issue any order seeking to achieve a racial balance in any school by requiring the transportation of pupils or students from one school to another or one school district to another in order to achieve such racial balance, or otherwise enlarge the existing power of the court to insure compliance with constitutional standards."

TITLE V

Commission on Civil Rights. Extends life of the Commission to January 31, 1968. Provides for procedural rules including at least 30 days public notice of Civil Rights Commission hearings. Entitles any person subpoenaed to appear before the Commission to bring along a lawyer, who may examine his client and make objections on the record. Requires the Commission, when it determines that testimony may tend to defame, degrade or incriminate any person, to receive it in executive session. Before such evidence can be used, the person affected has the right to testify in executive session and produce a reasonable number of witnesses. If the Commission then decides to release such evidence, it must be done at a public session, with opportunity for the defamed person to appear and be heard.

Empowers the Civil Rights Commission to serve as a national clearinghouse for information on denial of equal protection of the laws due to discrimination in fields including, but not limited to, voting, education, housing, employment, use of public facilities, transportation, and administration of justice.

TITLE VI

Nondiscrimination in Federally Assisted Programs. Bars discrimination on ground of race, color, or national origin in programs assisted by the Federal Government, excluding Federal insurance and guaranty programs. Authorizes and directs the assisting agency to effectuate non-discrimination by rules, regulations and orders of general applicability in Federally assisted projects with the agency action becoming effective only upon the approval of the President. Action by an agency under this title with respect to employment practices of an employer, employment agency or labor organization is restricted to situations "where a primary objective of the Federal financial assistance is to provide employment."

Authorizes termination of an assistance program in cases of noncompliance with the agency requirements, provided that compliance with the law cannot be obtained by voluntary means, and an express finding has been made on the record, after opportunity for hearing, of a failure to comply. Provides that notice of termination of assistance under this title and all pertinent facts of the case be submitted by the head of the Federal agency involved to the appropriate committees of the House of Representatives and of the Senate. No termination order would be effective until 30 days from the date the report is submitted to the appropriate Congressional committees. Agency action is subject to judicial review.

Equal Employment Opportunity. Applies to individuals, corporations, associations, partnerships, unincorporated organizations, and labor unions engaged in business affecting interstate commerce. Excludes employers who have less than 25 employees, private clubs, the U.S. and State governments, and religious and educational organizations with respect to work connected with their religious and educational activities.

Provides that this title becomes effective one year from the date of its enactment. Provides that for one year thereafter, businesses having fewer than 100 employees shall not be covered by this title; for the second year thereafter, businesses having fewer than 75 employees shall not be covered; for the third year thereafter, businesses having fewer than 50 employees shall not be covered; for the fourth year and thereafter, only businesses having fewer than 25 employees shall not be covered. Labor unions operating hiring halls are covered the year after enactment of the title. Unions generally are covered by the number of their members (100, 75,

50, 25) according to the same time sequence as set out for employers above.

Prohibits discrimination and segregation based on race, color, religion, sex or national origin in hiring practices, wages and conditions of employment, and employment opportunities. Prohibits discrimination in labor-union membership. Prohibits discrimination by employment agencies in referrals for employment. Prohibits discrimination against an employee because the employee has opposed practices prohibited by this title.

Expressly states it is not an unlawful practice for an employer, union or employment agency to act on the basis of "religion, sex, or national origin in those certain instances where religion, sex, or national origin is a bona fide occupational qualification reasonably necessary to the normal operation of that particular business or enterprise."

Creates an Equal Employment Opportunity Commission to be composed of five members, not more than three of whom shall be from the same political party. Members are to be appointed by the President with the advice and consent of the Senate.

Empowers the Commission to investigate charges of employment discrimination and "endeavor to eliminate any such alleged unlawful employment practice by informal methods of conference, conciliation, and persuasion." Charges may be brought in writing under oath by a person claiming to be aggrieved, or by written charge of a member of the Commission who has reasonable cause to believe a violation of the title has occurred, within 90 days of the alleged violation. In states that have fair employment laws prohibiting the practice alleged and establishing a state or local agency to handle such charges, charges may not be filed by an aggrieved person with the Commission until sixty days after the commencement of proceedings under local law (unless earlier terminated under state law), and charges filed by a member of the Commission may not be acted upon until sixty days after notice has been given to appropriate state or local authorities (120 days in either case during the first year after the effective date of such state or local law).

The period of 90 days from the date of violation within which a charge must be brought with the Commission is extended by the amount of time taken in resort to state and local agencies.

If the Commission is unable to obtain voluntary compliance with the title within 30 days (which may be extended to 60 days if the Commission determines that further compliance efforts are warranted), the person claiming to be aggrieved may sue for compliance in Federal court, and "the court may appoint an attorney for such complainant and may authorize the commencement of the action without the payment of fees, costs, or security." Where a member of the Commission has brought the original charge, the suit may be brought "by any person whom the charge alleges was aggrieved by the alleged unlawful employment practice." If the Attorney General certifies that the case is of general public importance, he may be permitted to intervene by the court. If the court finds that an unlawful employment practice has been committed it may enjoin the illegal conduct and order affirmative action, including reinstatement of hiring of employees, with or without back pay.

Authorizes the Attorney General to bring a civil action in Federal court seeking a permanent or temporary injunction where he has reasonable cause to believe that any person or group of persons is engaged in a pattern or practice of resistance to the enjoyment of the rights secured by the title. Authorizes the Attorney General to ask for a three-judge Federal court if he certifies the case "is of general public importance." Authorizes appeal from a three-judge court directly to the U.S. Supreme Court.

Authorizes the Commission to cooperate with and use the services of state and local agencies administering state fair employment practices laws, and enter into agreements with such state and local agencies ceding them jurisdiction in any case or class of classes.

Provides that employers covered by the act post notice of fair-employment-practice provisions of the act. Provides that the President, "as soon as feasible after the enactment of this title," convene one or more conferences to acquaint the leaders of groups who may be affected by this title with its provisions.

TITLE VIII

Registration and Voting Statistics. Orders the Secretary of Commerce to compile voting and voter-registration statistics for elections in which members of the House of Representatives have been nominated or elected since January 1, 1960, including age and race data, in areas recommended for survey by the Civil Rights Commission. A similar study is to be done in connection with the 1970 census. Provides that no person may be compelled to answer questions about his race, national origin, political affiliation, or how he voted.

TITLE IX

Intervention in Civil Rights Cases. Provides that the Attorney General may intervene in any civil suit for relief

134

from the denial of equal protection of the laws under the Fourteenth Amendment on account of race, color, religion, or national origin, if he certifies the case "is of general public importance."

TITLE X

Establishment of Community Relations Service. Establishes in the Department of Commerce a Community Relations Service, with a director appointed for a four-year term by the President with the advice and consent of the Senate. Empowers the Service to provide conciliation assistance to communities and persons "in resolving disputes, disagreements, or difficulties relating to discriminatory practices based on race, color, or national origin . . ." The Service may offer its services on its own motion or upon the request of an appropriate state official or other interested person. Provides that the Service "shall, whenever possible, in performing its functions, seek and utilize the co-operation of appropriate state or local, public, or private agencies." Provides that the Service's conciliation work be confidential and without publicity.

TITLE XI

Miscellaneous. Provides for jury trials, at demand of defendants, in criminal contempt proceedings arising under Titles II through VII (the section does not apply to contempts committed in the presence of the court, or nearby, or to misconduct of officers of the court in respect to writs, orders, or processes of the court). Under prior law, jury trials were already provided for contempt proceedings involving voting rights.

Provides for penalty, upon conviction for criminal contempt under Titles II through VII, of a fine of not more than $1,000 or imprisonment for not more than six months.

Bars trial for criminal contempt under the act if an acquittal or conviction has occurred in a prosecution for a specific crime under laws of United States based on the same act or omission of the defendant. Bars prosecution for a specific crime under laws of the United States if an acquittal or conviction has occurred in a proceeding for criminal contempt based upon the same act or omission of defendant.

INDEX

Abolitionists, 10.

Anderson, Marian, 70.

Architecture, Paul R. Williams and, 66-67.

Armed Forces, equal opportunities in, 90-92.

Athletics, Negroes participating in, 67-68.

Bethune, Mary McLeod, 31-32.

Biffle, Captain Richard L., 92.

Brown, Ensign Jessie L., 88-89.

Brown, John, 11-12.

Bunche, Dr. Ralph C., 48-49.

Carver, Dr. George Washington, as teacher, 30; as scientist, 61.

Chappelle, Emmett W., 99-100.

Civil Rights, organizations for, 111-119; progress in, 82; protest movements for, 101-111; state advisory committees, 25-26.

Civil Rights Acts, of 1957, 19-20; of 1960, 20; of 1962, 20; of 1964, 20, 81, 125-136 (Summary of 1964).

Colleges and Universities: Atlanta University, 29; Cookman Institute, 31; Fisk University, 29; Hampton Institute, 29; Howard University, 29, 34, 74; Lincoln University (Missouri), 34; Tuskegee Institute, 29; West Virginia State College, 34.

Commission on Civil Rights, creation of, 20; and housing opportunity, 78; membership of, 25; power of, 25; purpose of, 25.

Committee on Civil Rights, 24.

Compromise of 1850, 10.

Congress of Racial Equality (CORE), 111, 117; James Farmer, director, 105, 117.

Contributions by Negroes, in medicine, 64-65; music, 6, 68-72; science, 58-63.

Davis, Major General Benjamin O. (USAF), 92.

Dwight, Captain Edward D., 96.

Education, attendance in schools and colleges, 32-34; court decisions involving, 27-28, 39-40; de facto segregation in, 109-110; honors and achievement in, 34-39; Morrill Act of 1862, 30.

Eisenhower, President Dwight D., 91.

Emancipation Proclamation, 14-15.

Employment, labor unions and, 45-46; in major occupations, 43-44; sources of: advertising, 57; architecture, 66-67; armed forces, 58; athletics, 67; business, 56-57; education, 57; government, 46, 51-55; medicine, 63-66; music, 68-72; nursing, 66; science, 63-66.

Executive Orders, Presidential: No. 8802, 53-54; No. 9908, 24.

Explorations by Negroes in early America, 1.

Fair Employment Practice Laws, 55-56.

Farmer, James L., 117.

Fifteenth Amendment, 18.

Foreign Service, Negroes serving in, 51-52.

Fourteenth Amendment, 17-18, 23.

Free Negroes, 12-13.

Freedom for slaves, buying of, 8; desire for, 8; difficult to obtain, 8; risks of seeking, 9; Underground Railroad, 9-10.

Fugitive Slave Law, 10.